From Galley Boy to Tugmaster

Captain C.H. Noble. M.B.E.

Memoirs of a Hull Tugmaster.

Compiled by The United Towing & Salvage Society.

The United Towing & Salvage Society is a non-profit making organisation set up by former crew members with the aim of furthering the knowledge and memory of United Towing Company of Hull, and of the men who crewed the tugs and those who worked ashore.

Throughout this book we have used many photographs. Most of these were taken by crew members from the various tugs on scene at the time, where these individuals are known due credit has been given. Where images have been obtained from other sources in the public domain, for example the internet, we have credited the individuals who lay claim to their copyright at that source. On the few occasions that we have been unable to identify copyright owners from the source we have stated such.

Also, in researching certain historical facts we have taken information directly from the internet, particularly from sites such as Wrecksite.

We apologise for any possible infringement that may offend copyright owners but if they make their objections known to The United Towing & Salvage Society then we will ensure that any images and text are correctly credited, or removed entirely from any future editions of the book.

info@unitedtowingsociety.co.uk

www.unitedtowingsociety.co.uk

Copyright © 2017 The United Towing & Salvage Society

First published in Great Britain in 2017 by Black Tree Publishing

ISBN: 978-0-9955081-3-2

Published by Black Tree Publishing, Hull
Gemini House, Lee Smith Street Hull HU9 1SD
Telephone: 01482 328677

Printed by: Fisk Printers, Hull

Contents

Chapter 1
August 1945 - Steam tugs *Merman (1911)*, *Yorkshireman (1928)*

Merman (1911).

This was my very first tug, I'd left school at the age of fourteen unsure of what I wanted to do regarding employment, although I always had a feeling that I would like to go to sea, I think because my grandfather was in the Merchant Navy during the first world war. I never knew him though because his ship called *S/S Tummel* was torpedoed off Yarmouth. [1]

One day I wandered down to Hull Corporation pier which I often did just to watch ships come and go, also to look at the ferry boat that sailed back and forth to New Holland with cars and passengers. Then one day whilst visiting Corporation pier I noticed a small tug called *Merman* moored alongside the jetty end, so being interested I strolled over for a closer look.

The crew were sat on the engine room casing, all had large mugs of something, must have been tea or coffee, however they must have noticed me looking at them. Then a voice boomed out in a Scottish accent, "Are you alright son and are you interested in the boat?" I then replied "Yes." He then invited me aboard for a look round, they gave me one of those large mugs full of tea, I had to hold it with both hands. I was then asked "How old are you then? I replied "Fourteen." The skipper, called James Cowie, then asked "Would you like a job aboard?" I said " I'd love to," thinking he was kidding me, but he wasn't kidding, then I really didn't know what I was getting into. The skipper then said come with me. We both walked across the road and into a large office, written across the door of the office was a large sign saying United Towing Ltd. I then met the marine super and that's how I got my first job on tugs, what's more I had to start straight away. So along with Captain Cowie the tug skipper we returned back to the tug *Merman* - no sooner had we returned aboard, we got under way.

Merman (1911)
Photo UTSS collection.

[1] From Wrecksite.
NOBLE, Walter James Able Seaman MM SS Tummel (Hull) killed 24.2.16
SS Tummel, built by Goole Shipbuilding & Repairing Co. Ltd., Goole in 1912 and owned at the time of her loss by E. P. Hutchinson, Hull, was a British steamer of 531 tons.
On February 24th, 1916, on a voyage from Grimsby to Tréport with a cargo of coal, she was sunk by a mine from the German submarine UC-5 (Ulrich Mohrbutter), 7 miles south of the Kentish Knock light vessel, River Thames' mouth.
9 persons were lost.

I never had a clue where we were heading for, when I asked, they told me that we were going to Alexandra Dock jetty to take on coal. My first thought was that a coal lorry would come and put sacks of coal aboard like they did at home. I soon found out how.

After mooring alongside the coaling jetty, a large steel chute was lowered into the tug hatches then the coal came with a roar into the bunker hatch. To me, being green to the job it seemed tons upon tons came, I'd never seen so much coal in one go.

There was coal dust all over the tug including me when the hatches were full, some coal spilled out onto the deck, in fact quite a lot of it. However, the mate, a comic called Jackson shouted "What are you gawping at, grab a shovel," and myself and the rest of the crew started shovelling the coal that had spilled onto the deck into the tug bunkers.

We shovelled the coal for about an hour, hell I was as black as a Kentucky minstrel and more, I said to the mate "Can we have a rest?" he answered "Not until the hook is clear," I thought to myself what the hell is he talking about, the hook? It was then explained that the hook was where the tow rope went onto. However when the towing hook was cleared, the decks were washed down and we then proceeded towards Alexandra Dock.

Whilst entering the lock pits a chap wearing an old trilby shouted down to our skipper some orders, apparently he was the tugs broker called Harold, can't remember his second name. He shouted "Next tide skipper", the time now was six o'clock pm, I thought that we would be coming back to work next day, but I was in for quite a shock - apparently the next tide was three o'clock the next morning.

After entering the dock and mooring the *Merman* alongside, all hands aboard started going home. I was left standing on the tug's deck, then a voice shouted "Pass our bikes up to us son." So one by one I passed the bikes ashore, five altogether. I then asked "What do I do now?" the mate answered "Get yourself home and be back on board at two o'clock sharp." I said "You mean early morning?" They all laughed and said "Oh yes because you have to come aboard one hour before the rest of the crew to trim the navigation lights and light them, plus light the galley fire." Also the second engineer had to come early to raise steam.

So there I was filthy and hungry, I had no money and wasn't quite sure where I was. However I got my bearings and headed home walking. So from Alexandra Dock to home which was then North Hull Estate, I think. Looking back it took me about an hour and a half to walk. As I entered our house the first greeting was "Where the hell have you been all day?" "And just look at the state you're in." That was my mother, my brother Tom started laughing, I was still black from the coal dust, my father just sat there grinning. I blurted out "I've got a job on a tug." Dad then said "Shall you be getting paid?"

Just after midnight next morning I set off walking back to Alexandra Dock, I was very tired, but I intended to carry on to my first job, another hour and a half walk. I finally climbed aboard the *Merman*, I couldn't see anybody, everything was pitch black. Then a head popped up from the engine room hatch, it was the second engineer called Bert Cooper, nice chap, his father was a tug skipper. However Bert, second engineer, took me under his wing, he said "Never expected to see you again!"

He then told me what I had to do, first rake out the ash from the galley fire grate, then get a handful of cotton waste, then soak the waste in paraffin, drop the soaked waste into the grate then put some chunks of coal onto the waste, then stand back and throw a match onto it, which I did, and with a large whoosh away it went, galley fire lit. Next job fill a large kettle from a hand pump inside the galley, I then said to Bert "What next, is that it?" he laughed and said "No way, you now have to trim and light the navigation lights, consisting of two masthead lights, one port light, one starboard light, plus a stern light, fill them with paraffin and light them." I remember it very well because to light them I used a roll of newspaper sticking one end into the galley fire then trying to be quick light each and every one, burning my finger ends.

Three o'clock came and the rest of the crew came aboard. Their first words were, "Have you mashed up yet?" I said "The kettle's boiling." I was then shown a large tea kettle, it was huge, it held seven pints of water. I put four large tablespoons of tea into the kettle and made the tea. So that was another job I had to do. Then another crew member explained that I hadn't lit the cabin fire, but Bert the second told them to do it themselves. I think the crew were breaking me in gently, so that was my first twenty four hours on tugs.

I must say those early days were very rough indeed, but then again to me, at fourteen, it was a great adventure, (that was to last the next fifty years). Whilst being on the *Merman* we amused ourselves by raiding barges that were moored inside the dock, mind you we only did this between tides when the rest of the crew went home, and what I mean by the word us meant other deck boys from other tugs. To us it wasn't worth going home because in those days we had to work every tide, during daylight hours we used to swim in the dock, then under dark hours we used to borrow small boats called coggie boats from barges, then go from barge to barge lifting the hatch covers for a look see.

These barges were loaded with practically everything, mostly food such as tinned fruit, cases of dried eggs, corned beef. After storing our loot on board the tug, we took the coggie boat back to the barge that we had borrowed it from, we lived a life of luxury, the only food we bought was bread. I remember my first pay packet which was the grand total of £1.50 of today's money per week, a seven day week and almost twelve to fourteen hours a day, but we never grumbled, we just got on with it.

I spent about three months aboard the tug *Merman* as a deck boy, after that I set my eyes on the larger tugs. So one day whilst collecting my pay at the office I asked the boss, a Captain Copperthwait, if he could put my name down for a sea going tug because I had seen two large tugs moored inside Railway dock which was the town docks in Hull.

They had just come back from war service with the Royal Navy, one was called *Seaman* and the other was called *Superman*. They were still painted grey and were waiting for a refit before handing back to United Towing for peacetime working. I was promised a galley boy's job aboard the tug *Seaman* when she had completed her refit which was to take at least three months.

I was then told by the office that I could join a tug called *Yorkshireman* which was stationed at Grimsby and was still under contract with the government. I was dead chuffed, here I was fourteen and a half, a fully fledged sailor! Also I owned a posh suit, and most of all I was now mobile, I'd purchased a second hand bike because I thought I would have to bike to Grimsby but no, I was given a railway ticket which would take me via the New Holland ferry and onto Grimsby docks. So with my belongings which wasn't much, I made my way to the tug *Yorkshireman*.

Yorkshireman (1928)

Yorkshireman (1928)
Photo UTSS collection.

After searching the dock I found *Yorkshireman* moored outside the dock alongside the jetty which was her permanent berth. When I first saw her I thought she was a warship because she was painted all grey and had two small guns, mounted on each wing of the bridge, her wooden decks were snow white. At first I was scared to go aboard, I thought I'd made a mistake. I just stood there on the jetty top with my kit (an ex flour bag) that was stuffed with my jeans, shoes etc. I was wearing my war time clogs. However, I wasn't there long before a booming voice shouted "Is your name Noble?" I replied "Yes sir" the voice came from the *Yorkshireman's* mate, a man called Alf Varley who in later years became a tug Captain himself. He said "Don't stand there all day, get yourself aboard." Once aboard I thought hell this is posh. After being aboard the tug *Merman*, *Yorkshireman* was more like a yacht than a tug, reason being she was built to take on passengers in and out of Bridlington during the summer season, then she reverted back to towing duties during winter months. I was shown to my cabin which turned out to be the ladies saloon, very posh it was. It had large settees which I used to sleep on, gee I felt like royalty, never been used to anything like this, even had a wash basin and a flushing toilet. Whilst aboard the *Merman* all we had for washing was a bucket for everything.

Next day the *Yorkshireman's* skipper, a man called Sheriff, took me to the local shipping office in Grimsby to sign on the ships articles as a deck boy. They took my finger prints, then measured me, five foot, six and a half inches, then photographed me. After all that I was presented with a Merchant Navy identity card complete with photo and finger prints plus a seaman's ration book and also a book of clothing coupons. Clothes were still rationed.

As a bonus I was given a Merchant Navy silver badge to wear in my suit lapel, gee I thought I was somebody. The reason we were given a ration book and clothing book was because seamen were given twice as much rations and clothing coupons than civilians because of the sea clothing a seaman had to buy. I found out later some seamen just sold their clothing books for booze and cigarettes.

However back aboard the *Yorkshireman* I started to have a good look around, I smelt cooking from the galley and looked in sniffing, the cook then said "Hi, have you got anything to cook?" I just stood there not too sure what he meant, then I was told that the *Yorkshirman's* crew had to provide their own food and the cook's job was to cook whatever they gave him, but the cook knocked up a meal for me anyway. It was two slices of corned beef and mash potato.

After the meal he lent me some money so I could go shopping. After getting permission from the skipper I ventured ashore. Whilst walking down the dock side I saw what looked like a large warehouse come shop. Royal Navy personnel were coming out carrying bags of what looked like shopping, so in I went for a look. It turned out it was a Naffi store and run by WRENS, Women's Royal Navy. At the counter a WREN asked if she could help me, I in turn said "Could I purchase some food stores?"

They looked me up and down and said "Are you in the Royal Navy son?" and started laughing. I told the WRENS that I had just joined the large tug called *Yorkshireman* as a deck boy and that I had to feed myself. They then said "Sorry this store is only for Royal Navy personnel." I was about to walk away when I noticed the WRENS started to whisper amongst themselves. It was then they told me to go around to the back of the warehouse which I did and, surprise, surprise they gave me two large bags of slightly damaged goods consisting of tins of you name it, it was there, even broken bars of chocolate. I could hardly carry them but did not have far to walk back to the *Yorkshireman*.

On arrival I met the cook and gave him his money back which I had borrowed earlier before going ashore. He was amazed at what I had. He and the crew called me a crafty little so-n-so. After that I started giving the cook a pound note every week to keep me fed, mind you I shared my given spoils with him.

After a few days I settled in quite well. I liked the crew but Alf Varley was a hard working mate and expected us to follow suit. Every morning the decks had to be scrubbed clean, then breakfast. After breakfast it was painting or chipping rust with chipping hammers.

So now I've got a confession to make from all those years ago! One day a wooden stage was rigged over the starboard side of *Yorkshireman's* bow, myself and a deckhand were seated on this stage chipping rust and paint. As I remember my hands were freezing cold, the other deckhand went to make some tea. I was left on the stage. I was rubbing my hands to keep them warm, I then noticed a steel ladder running down the side of the jetty, so, making sure that nobody was looking, I decided to accidentally fall in the water and grab the rung of the ladder, at the same time shouting help.

The mate Alf Varley and other members of the crew dragged me out of the cold water, stripped my clothes off, and found that I was not hurt in any way. I finished up sat in the galley with a blanket around me and also given a large mug of cocoa. The skipper told Alf Varley off for putting a young lad over the side on a working stage without a life jacket. No comment!

A few days later I asked a crew member, "When are we supposed to go to sea?" He started laughing, then told me we was just on stand by in case the tug was needed. Apparently mine sweepers were clearing mines up and down the east coast between Flamborough Head and the Humber and if any accidents happened *Yorkshireman* went to their assistance, but apart from that the *Yorkshireman* sailed to the Humber and Spurn light vessels every Thursday to supply fresh water and food stores if needed.

Sometimes we went to the Bull Fort which was manned by the army. *Yorkshireman* was ideal for this because she was shallow drafted. Once when we were alongside Bull Fort I got permission to go onto the fort for a look round. There were about twenty soldiers there, also a large gun pointing seawards. I noticed that the accommodation was very rough to me, the heating was paraffin heaters. I think by 1946 the forts were abandoned. They're just there now like old war relics.

I spent about eight weeks aboard the *Yorkshireman*, then one day we received orders to return to Hull. The Ministry of Defence had handed the *Yorkshireman* back to the owners United Towing Ltd. On arrival at Hull the *Yorkshireman* moored alongside the ocean going tug *Seaman*. Being a Friday we all paid off and went home. All the crew to report to the office for further orders, mine being to join the *Seaman* as a galley/cabin boy.

Chapter 2
1946 - *Seaman (1924)* / Empire Tugs

Gee, at the time I felt honoured, but *Seaman* was still having a refit so every day was spent working by the tug cleaning and painting over the dark grey paint that she was painted in during the war years. Each day different faces began appearing aboard, the office sent tugmen aboard to work by until other tugs could be found for them, and some of these men worked on the tugs during the war. During tea breaks down in the after cabin, that's the accommodation for firemen and deckhands, (officers lived in posh accommodation up at the forward end of the tug), I used to sit in a corner practically out of sight just listening to their yarns about their experiences during the war.

Seaman (1924)
Photo UTSS collection.

First yarn was about a sea tug called *Englishman,* built before the war. However, she was stationed at Cambletown, Scottish Islands along with the *Seaman.* They were always on standby to assist any merchant vessel that was in trouble such as being torpedoed or engine failing. Apparently one night *Englishman* was called to assist some vessel in trouble, the next day she sent out a distress call saying she was being attacked by a German aircraft. After that call nothing more was heard. She was lost with all hands, the skipper's name was George Spence. In later years I visited the war memorial at Tower Hill and it was there that I saw *Englishman's* name wrote upon it.

Englishman (1938)
Photo UTSS collection.

I used to love these tea break yarns. The next yarn was about *Seaman* herself, ears pricked up I listened. As I have mentioned *Seaman* was also stationed at Cambletown and was called out for salvage and rescue duties. A ship had been bombed by German aircraft and *Seaman* was on her way to assist. Whilst approaching the vessel a German fighter bomber (a Foch-Wolf Condor) was machine gunning the vessel in distress. Apparently he may have had no bombs left, we don't really know for sure, but when the German aircraft spotted the *Seaman* it turned its attention to her and dived towards her with guns blazing.

Now, during the war, *Seaman* had two guns, one on either side of her bridge. The yarn goes that the mate of the *Seaman* called Jacky Ryan was manning one of these guns and he started firing at the German aircraft. As it swept low over the tug he never thought that he would do any good but, lo and behold, a 'hit.' The German aircraft crashed into the Atlantic. The story goes that *Seaman* managed to rescue the pilot. Once on board some crew members wanted to beat him up because they had friends on the *Englishman*. However, he was brought ashore back at Cambletown and handed over to army personnel. Jacky Ryan, I was told, was awarded a medal, I believe he got the George Cross [2], but funny enough a couple of days later Jack Ryan came aboard to work by. I asked if the story was true and he confirmed it. He also showed me an indent in front of *Seaman's* wireless room from one of the German cannon shells. That indent was never repaired.

James (Jack) Ryan GM
Photo copyright Sue Shillito.

[2] From The London Gazette 4th February 1941.

To be an Additional Officer of the Civil Division of the Most Excellent Order of the British Empire:—
Captain Owen Vincent Jones, Master.

Awarded the George Medal:— James Ryan, First Mate. The ship was attacked by an enemy aircraft, which came upon her from astern, circled round and three times attacked her from ahead. Mr. Ryan, at his gun, held his fire until the last moment and brought down the aircraft. Meanwhile, the Master, Captain Jones, out-manoeuvred the enemy, and his good seamanship undoubtedly helped to save the ship.

Foche-Wolf Condor
Photo copyright unknown – Public domain.

Empire tugs.

At the beginning of the war United Towing was having two sea going tugs built but the government took them over after completion and renamed one *Empire Oak* and the other *Empire Larch*. *Empire Oak* was the first to be completed and her duties were escorting merchant ships in convoy. On one occasion she was escorting a convoy from the UK towards Gibraltar, several ships were torpedoed and sunk. *Empire Oak* picked up some of the survivors but sadly she too was torpedoed, but as the story goes she was steaming alongside an oil tanker and they believe the torpedo that sank *Empire Oak* was meant for the oil tanker, who knows! [3]

Years later I was mate with the Captain of the lost *Empire Oak*, his name was Captain Christian, however, when *Empire Larch* was ready for sea Captain Christian took command of her and sailed thousands of miles in her. After the war years United Towing reclaimed the *Empire Larch* and renamed her *Masterman*.

Most of United Towing sea tugs were ex-Empire tugs. *Empire Bess* became *Merchantman*, *Empire Julia* became *Tradesman*, *Empire Nina* became *Guardsman*, *Empire Stella* became *Serviceman*. *Empire Stella* was bought by United Towing minus a boiler and engines because her boiler blew up and destroyed her engine and killed some of her crew whilst towing barges in the Thames Estuary. So United Towing put new boilers plus new engines into her and she sailed for many years ocean towing. She was later converted to a diesel tug with increasing power.

Merchantman (1946) *[Empire Bess 1946]*
Photo UTSS collection.

Serviceman (1946) *[Empire Stella 1945]*
Photo UTSS collection.

Tradesman (1946) *[Empire Julia 1944]*
Photo UTSS collection.

Guardsman (1947) *[Empire Nina 1946]*
Photo UTSS collection.

[3] From Wrecksite
Empire Oak was a British Steam Tug of 484 tons built in 1941. On the 22nd August 1941 when on route from Methil Roads for Gibraltar she was torpedoed by German submarine *U-564* and sunk.
The master, three crew members and four gunners from the *Empire Oak* (Master Frederick Edward Christian) were picked up by *HMS Campanula* (K 18) (Lt.Cdr R.V.E. Case, DSC), transferred to *HMS Velox* (D 34) (Lt.Cdr E.G. Ropner DSC) and landed at Gibraltar on 25 August. 13 crew members were lost.
On 19 August, the *Empire Oak* had picked up six survivors from *Aguila* and eleven survivors from *Alva*. The survivors from *Aguila* died when this ship was sunk, while the other survivors were also rescued by the corvette.

Voyage to Africa.

However, back to my early days on *Seaman*. After working by the *Seaman* for four weeks it was time for sailing. The cook joined, an ex-fisherman called Samson and it was him that said to me "How would you like to go to Africa son?" Course as a young lad I was overjoyed, so next day all *Seaman's* crew went to the shipping office in Posterngate in Hull to sign on for the coming voyage. I signed on as cabin boy. Back on board all hands started loading stores.

There were sack upon sack of potatoes plus cases of all sorts, then I noticed some joiner erecting two large casks, looked like large beer barrels, one either side of the lower bridge deck. Then when he had finished the cook passed me a new bucket and he had one for himself, then we both started filling these large barrels up with water. After the barrels were full the cook started shovelling rock salt into the barrels, I said "What are they for?" He replied "They are for keeping meat in for the voyage ahead." He told me to get a potato, he then threw the potato into the barrel and waited a few seconds, sure enough the potato floated to the surface. Then we started packing loads of fresh meat into each barrel, so that's when I realised the *Seaman* never had a fridge.

Next day was coaling day so we sailed from the Town Docks to Alexandra Dock jetty to take on bunker coal. I have never seen so much coal in my life, wagons upon wagons of coal came aboard. I thought to myself when is it going to stop. Well it did for a short period whilst the crew battened the hatches down, then it all started again. Forty tons of coal was then dropped onto the decks, reason being that when the fireman or stokers used up some coal during the voyage the idea was to shovel the coal that was on deck into the bunkers.

There was water lapping onto the decks but with me being green at the time I thought all was normal, but I now realise that the *Seaman* was overloaded. We sailed at night time, I think the case was so no official could witness the state she was in. To get from the aft cabin to the forward end of the tug you either climbed a mountain of coal or went via the engine room.

We sailed at about midnight. After washing dishes etc. I went to my bunk which was down the aft cabin. My bunk was situated over the tug's propeller, hell what a noise it made, like a large swishing sound, but I was so tired I fell asleep soundly.

During the night the *Seaman* was pitching and rolling, I couldn't get to sleep again, so I wedged myself with a life-jacket and then fell sound asleep. I'm not sure how long I had been asleep but I awoke to find everything was still and quiet. The lights were out and I could hear water splashing. I put my hand over the side of my bunk and felt water. I then panicked and climbed out of my bunk only to disappear under water. However, I managed to surface and find the steps leading to the deck. The hatch was broken so as I climbed out on deck I noticed that most of the coal that was on deck when we sailed had been washed aft and overboard. I stumbled towards the galley which was situated amidships and inside the galley found most of the crew. As I walked in they sang out "Oh here he is!" Apparently they thought I'd gone missing. The *Seaman* was now anchored inside Yarmouth roads sheltering and clearing the steering gear aft where some of the coal had washed. All the sailors bedding and belongings were wet through and were drying on the boiler top and that's where I finished my nap.

After breakfast next day it was up anchor and away for Africa, a port called Lagos. After crossing the Bay of Biscay the weather and sea was perfect, blue sky and calm sea. It was nice to sit out on deck peeling spuds, a bucket full every day, and washing dishes in the same bucket. Also using the same bucket to wash myself and my clothes.

Apparently all hands had their own bucket for this purpose as there was no bathroom aboard. To get a bath you had to go down the engine room and fill your bucket with condensed water from the steam engine, go into the stoke hold where the firemen were throwing coal into the furnace, lather yourself with soap then tip the rest of the water over your head. That's how you bathed yourself, that's the way things were in them days.

One day the cook said to me "You're leaving me for a while because you are needed in the coal bunkers." I couldn't understand just what he meant but I was soon to find out. The coal was too far back inside the bunkers for the stokers to reach with their shovels, so I was lowered through the bunker hatch into the bunkers. Then a steel wheelbarrow was lowered after me, plus a shovel which, at the time, was larger than me.

My job now was as a trimmer which meant me filling the wheelbarrow with coal then pushing the barrow towards the opening which led to the stokehold. Then tip the barrow of coal into the opening so that the stokers could feed the fires. This I did for hours on end, my arms were like lumps of lead. I was as black as the coal itself. This went on for days, in fact I finished up sleeping in the coal bunkers. I had an old mattress that I had laid on top of a bed of coal dust.

After shovelling and barrowing coal for the stokers I used to lay down on this mattress for a sleep, but whatever time it was night or day the stokers, if they wanted more coal, they just pelted a lump of coal at my bed. And so it started again, back to my barrow. I felt like the story of Tom and the chimney sweep, I was black and dirty and I developed a polished shine all over my body.

However, *Seaman* arrived at the Azores and anchored to take on bunkers and fresh water, oh and lots of fresh fruit because we needed it. The only sort of fruit we had was concentrated lime juice with water. As for meat, during the voyage to the Azores it made me sick just to get it out of the wooden casks. What I had to do was reach inside with the aid of a boat hook, stab a meat joint, drop it into a pan of boiling water until cooked, then the crew had to eat the stuff. They said that it tasted okay but I wouldn't touch it, no way.

We stocked up again in the Azores.

Now that the coal bunkers were full again I was a cabin boy again scrubbing out cabins and back to my spud peeling again. It was good to be back on deck again after living in the coal bunkers, but it wasn't long before I was promoted to cook! The cook had gone sick and took to his bunk. Now what the hell did I know about cooking? But come to my rescue was the second engineer, a nice bloke called Billy Bass. He showed me what to do, especially when it came to making bread and currant duff puddings with bits of coal stuck on.

Bill Bass, 2nd Engineer.
Photo Keith Bass.

Our next port of call was Freetown where once again *Seaman* topped up with coal and fresh water. It took three days to take on bunkers because the coal was brought aboard in small baskets by men and women, carried on their heads. They were chanting some tune and were very happy at what they were doing.

We sailed again and this time the cook presented himself for duty in the galley so I was demoted back to a galley boy. Whilst on our stay in Freetown I purchased a handbag to take home as a present for my mother, it was brightly decorated with beads. I put it in my locker but days later I had a sneak look at it and, to my horror, all the so called beads had sprouted long shoots. They were beans painted over! I was learning slowly I think.

At last *Seaman* arrived in Lagos. It was scorching hot as I remember. It wasn't possible to sleep below decks. We tried sleeping on deck but were bitten all over by flying insects, so we had to sleep below again and sweat it out. Next morning we were surrounded by bum boats. For those that don't know what bum boats are, well they are canoes - small boats filled with goods for sale, such as fruit, cheap bangles, souvenirs, parrots, monkeys and birds in cages. I took a fancy to a little monkey so I had to start to barter a price for it. After a while we had a deal - two tins of corned beef, a pair of old trousers and a round tin of 50 cigarettes. Now I was the proud owner of a monkey.

Sangara, Lagos to Newcastle.

Anchored nearby a merchant vessel called *Sangara* was to be our tow back home. Her owners were Elder Dempster of Liverpool and the story was that she had been torpedoed during the Second World War. To save the ship the captain had managed to beach her onto a beach near Lagos. She was then abandoned and left with no hope of salvage, but the story goes that some mining engineers bought the wreck and, doing some patching up, managed to re-float her and furthermore sold *Sangara* back to her previous owners at a great profit. You can understand the Elder Dempster Company for wanting her back because she wasn't that old a ship and what's more there was a vast shortage of merchant ships after the war because so many had been sunk during the war and were hard to come by, and so was steel for building new ships.

A few days were spent in Lagos getting *Sangara* ready for sea and storing ourselves up with fresh stores and meat for our barrels on the bridge. Some said the meat was buffalo but it didn't bother me, I wouldn't eat any of it.

One early morning we set sail with *Sangara* in tow from Lagos harbour to the open sea where our long sea tow rope was paid out. Now this was the first time that I had seen a deep sea tow rope going out, it seemed never ending. A hundred and twenty fathoms of rope, sixteen inches circumference plus seventy fathoms of four inch wire attached to the end of the rope. Away we went, our final destination was to be Newcastle on the east coast of Britain.

Sangara
Photo T.W. Wards Shipbreakers, Preston, by Preston Digital Archive.

Whilst we were at Lagos the crew relaxed and sunbathed. One particular fireman overdid it and was a bright red on his chest and back. When it was his turn to go on watch all hell broke loose down the stoke hold and engine room. The *Seaman's* boiler had three fires and the fire door was opened for the fireman to throw a shovel full of coal into it, that's when he let out a scream. The heat from the fires came in contact with his sunburnt chest and he was in great pain. Also Billy Bass, the second engineer, was giving him a right rollicking for being so stupid. Guess what, I was promoted again, only this time instead of just trimmer I was fireman and trimmer. So, saying goodbye to the cook, I descended below.

The burnt fireman helped the cook. Learning to shovel coal into a fire whilst the boat was rolling is a work of art, but after a while I managed it with Billy Bass's encouragement. It was hard work raking out ashes, cooling them down then putting the cooled ashes into ash bags, then hauling the bags onto the deck and dumping them overboard. After four hours it was good to get back on deck. That's where I was sleeping now, (plus monkey).

One night whilst sleeping on deck I awoke to the sound of the engines and propeller slowing down. I laid there for a while then ventured towards the engine room hatch and noticed three engineers were discussing amongst themselves, and the skipper George Collier was down there as well. The steam engines were just about turning over. I then found out that the boilers tubes were leaking badly and the boiler was losing a lot of steam. So, listening to the conversation that was going on, I heard Billy Bass say "I will do it."

Now this meant raking the centre fire out completely then the two wing fires kept as small as possible, then they soaked old ash bags in sea water, laid them inside the middle fire box, then to my dismay I saw Billy Bass soak himself with water. Hand full of spanners, also a rope attached to his leg, then in the middle fire box he crawled inside whilst others paid out the rope. He was gone for about ten minutes then they pulled him out. I thought he had finished repairing but no he gulped a jug of cold water, discussed something with the other engineers and back in he went. After some time he came out and gasped, "All finished" he looked like a roasted pig. He stumbled out onto the deck to cool off, both his arms were blistered.

After bandaging his arms he was back on watch and raising full steam again. How I admired that man, I remained friends with Bill for years to come. Mind you on that same voyage if I was at all cheeky to him he gave me a clip across my ears or a kick up the backside, that was Billy Bass.

Later on in the voyage I was permanently stuck down below in the bunkers. The coal that we got in Lagos was rubbish, it was mainly just like coal dust. As the fireman threw the coal into the fires it more or less went straight up the funnel and wasn't any good for making steam. So myself along with other crew members started separating the coal dust from lumps of coal, hell it was work, with the heat the sweat just poured out of us. We must have swallowed quite a lot of coal dust. I remember the captain on board *Sangara* our tow saying "When are we going to get more speed?" our captain explained the situation with a few harsh words.

We plodded along, food was starting to get short, mainly the fresh. We had used all the veg and meat from the casks. But daily, flying fish used to land aboard, more so at night, they used to glide towards the *Seaman's* deck lights. So each morning we used to collect them all up and have a fry up for breakfast. Mind you we had to be quick because my monkey loved them too. Sometimes when a fish landed on board wriggling about on deck the monkey pounced, grabbed the fish then up the rigging it ran and ate it.

The day came when we arrived at Las Palmas and once again anchoring the tow we started taking on fresh stores and coal. Some of the crew had to go and see the doctor. Most of the stokers and engineers were covered in a rash and had to be treated, apparently it was just sweat rash and lack of fresh food that had caused it. We stayed a night in Las Palmas, our first night in port since we left Lagos. In Lagos it wasn't worth going ashore so the crew made the most of it, thick heads next morning. Next morning after reconnecting to the *Sangara* we sailed. Lovely calm sea it was, plenty of fresh food and everyone was in good spirits.

Whilst we were in Las Palmas some of the lads bought canaries, little yellow birds in wicker baskets. Now that the lads had sobered up they found all they had bought were sparrows dipped in yellow dye! So, still being in sight of land the birds were let loose and flew away.

So now I was back in the galley as a galley boy again. We were making good speed as I remember. I used to love just sitting on deck peeling my spuds, flat calm sea, watching dolphins swimming close by. Up till then I had never seen a dolphin before. Also Portuguese man-o-wars, these were names given to a jelly fish that had small like sails protruding from the main jelly fish. They were a bright purple colour and just drifted about in the wind.

I'm afraid the weather wasn't going to last. The wireless operator, a lovely man called Bob Depress, said there was going to be some very bad weather heading our way. So hatches were battened down.

I believe we were approaching somewhere between Cape St. Vincent and Cape Finisterre, not quite sure really. During the night the gale was upon us, storm force winds and very heavy seas head on from the north. All *Seaman* could do was reduce speed to take the strain off the towing wire, but at the same time we were making no headway, in fact we were blown astern.

After a few days the weather decreased and *Seaman* started to make some headway again, but worry was that we were burning a lot of coal. To make matters worse at Cape Finisterre we ran into a storm again. So now we were into the Bay of Biscay riding the storm out day by day.

As before I was promoted to trimmer again because the coal situation was starting to get desperate. There I was wheeling my barrow of coal backwards and forwards keeping the firemen supplied. The coal bunker now seemed more like a cathedral to me. There wasn't a lot of coal left, we finished up sweeping the bunkers sides. However, after a full week the gales eased and we started making headway again. With a stern wind we eventually arrived at Falmouth in Cornwall with very little coal left to burn.

As I remember *Seaman* stayed a few days in Falmouth for some repairs. We bunkered up with stores and good Welsh coal, then away we went all in good spirits. It didn't take long before we eventually arrived off the River Tyne at Newcastle. Four local tugs came out to take over the tow.

After heaving our towing gear aboard the local Tyne tugs towed the *Sangara* close by the *Seaman* and lined up on her decks were the captain and about a dozen African crew members. They all took off their woolly hats and *Sangara's* captain shouted "Three cheers for the tug *Seaman*" and all shouted "Hip-hip-hooray." Then one huge African shouted "And a big cheer for de fireman."

So *Seaman* headed back to Hull and we went on leave for about four days. United Towing wasn't very generous when it came to time off, then again just after the war they were very busy and were the only tug company in Europe at the time.

Well that's how it was, my first long sea trip on tugs. Me and monkey made our way home. First thing the monkey did was to jump onto the fireguard and wee into the fire, so that ended the voyage completely.

"Block ship", Arromanches to Blyth.

After our four days we reported back on board of the *Seaman* only to find that we were off to sea again. This time we were bound for Arromanches off the French coast. Now, during and after the D-Day invasion of France a temporary harbour was made using old merchant ships. What they did was, starting from the beach they sank the old ships in a large horse shoe fashion. I should think about thirty ships altogether to make some sound. Some were filled with concrete in barrels so it could be taken out again at a later stage, it was a clever idea. After they were grounded they were still above water so any small vessel could moor alongside of them. They were called "block ships" but now with the war over these block ships were raised and towed to the U.K. for scrap because there was a big demand for scrap metal at that time.

However, *Seaman* connected to one of these salvaged ships and commenced towing to Blythe on the east coast. Painted on the bows of these ships were the letters B.I.S.C.O. and a number after these letters, reason for this was, British Iron And Steel Corporation, the logo was the then nationalised steel of the U.K. which had purchased them from their previous owners. First couple of days went well then we noticed a slight list. As the voyage proceeded the list got steadily worse. By this time we were close to the River Humber so our skipper decided to beach the ship, now called "B.I.S.C.O. No. 1."

After grounding and recovering our sea gear, pumps were transferred and we pumped the vessel dry at low water. It was noticed there was a crack in the ships side, this was welded up and on the incoming tide she was re-floated and we proceeded to Blythe for scrap. After handing the vessel to local tugs we set sail again for Arromanches and repeated the performance, only this time the next tow was taken to Glasgow for scrap, again with no problems.

Towing these block ships from Arromanches was a regular job for *Seaman* and took quite a few months to clear. We finished up back in Hull for a few weeks mainly berthing tankers onto Saltend and Killingholme oil jetty's. Then *Seaman* was off again, this time we were bound for Germany to a port called Kiel.

Europa. Kiel to Firth of Forth.

Now Kiel was on the other end of the Kiel canal which is quite wide and deep. I'm not quite sure, I believe it's about ninety miles long. It was very interesting steaming through it, bridges and locks along the way. It was wide enough for two ships to pass each other.

On arrival at Kiel there was wrecks everywhere, lots of burnt out shells of ships from the war. Our tow was a large burnt out passenger ship called "Europa" which had been used for carrying German troops, but this tow needed two tugs so we waited for one of United Towing's tugs called *Brahman* to arrive.

Whilst waiting for *Brahman* to arrive we ventured ashore. British troops were everywhere and bombed out buildings everywhere. The locals were practically starving. For instance, for a carton of cigarettes you may get a gold watch, and for a pound of coffee beans you could name your own price, such as cameras and binoculars, it went on and on. Kids used to come aboard practically begging for food, such was Germany just after the war.

Anyhow both tugs now connected to the *Europa* plus a couple of German tugs. We then proceeded through the Kiel canal and so out into the North sea. As far as I can remember *Europa* was towed to a scrap yard on the Firth of Forth in Scotland.

Europa
Photo copyright unknown – Public domain.

Chapter 3
1946 - *R. W. Wheeldon (19XX) [Cabral (1912)]*.

These tows from the continent went on for almost two years. There were floating dry docks plus a few U-boats, Germany was practically drained of scrap metal. During these tows I spent most of my time as a deckhand although I was still signed on as a galley boy, so I went to our office asking for a deckhands job. I was given a deckhands job aboard a docking tug called *R.W. Wheeldon*. It was also my fifteenth birthday that day, I thought to myself that's a funny name for a tug. Apparently one of United Towing's former Directors was called R.W. Wheeldon, but, stranger still was the tug was an ex whale chasing ship converted to a tug. [4]

She looked ugly to me and yes she was a coal burmer, also paraffin lights to trim, but there was also another deckhand aboard so trimming lights was shared between us. She had the usual open bridge that the dock tugs had and two life boats. Looking inside these life boats they were half full of coal, so when the tug took coal aboard lots sprayed over onto the life boats and nobody had bothered to clean them out. But to me a fifteen year old kid I just thought it was the thing to do, such was United Towing's early days.

Every tug that went coasting around the British Isles had to carry a wind up radio for distress purposes, but it turned out only one of these radios was to serve half a dozen tugs, so if a tug was having a survey done, this radio was put aboard for the Lloyds surveyor to inspect and pass, but when the surveyor had passed it then the radio was taken off and put in United's stores ready for the next tug that had a survey!

R. W. Wheeldon
Photo UTSS collection.

[4] R. W. Wheeldon was one of the founder shareholders of United Towing Ltd., being part owner of City Steam Towage. He became a Hull councilor and later Lord Mayor of the City.

New built barges, Hull to London.

Whilst aboard *"Wheeldon"* we did dock work tide after tide, weekends off, no way! You couldn't make a date with anyone it was just impossible to do. Then I noticed a coil of sea tow rope covered over with tarpaulin, so asking what it was for, I was told it's for when we go to sea. I said you must be kidding, go to sea in this tug! But I'm afraid they were right. I found out for sure one evening when we had finished the tide, orders came saying, next tide early morning and fetch four days food with you because *R.W. Wheeldon* is going to tow two barges to London.

These were new barges built at Selby for the London river. A small tug called *Boatman* had brought the two barges down river in the morning and we took over to tow them to London. So, after bunkering up with coal we set to rigging the barges for sea, we were to tow them tandem fashion. First we had to put battery lights aboard of them, lug six large batteries on board that had come from the stores. After all I was only fifteen and my mate was only seventeen, it was hard work but we did it.

All rigged and ready to go we set off down river towards Spurn. At Spurn we streamed out the sea gear and away we went. The mate told us to trim our paraffin navigation lights, then I found out we had to trim and light a compass light.

Our watches were set, we did four hours on the bridge, four hours off. The skipper, Les Dawson was his name, said "Can you steer?" I replied "Yes," after all I'd come off the *Seaman*. Then he said "Can you box the compass?" I knew what he meant (do I know my compass?) I replied "Yes." He looked a bit surprised. I'd also learnt it on the *Seaman*. He said "You will be on watch with me."

When I eventually went on watch, first job was to light all the navigation lights, plus this little compass light which kept blowing out in the wind, so I had to light the compass light inside the galley, cover it under my old army coat then seat it on the compass binnacle, but it was very dim, you could hardly see the compass. I finished up shining a torch to see the compass more clearly. So on watch first I went with the skipper wrapped up in an old army great coat and a woollen bobble hat, God I was freezing cold, stood still for four hours in an open bridge with sea spray coming over the bow and spraying me. Every now and then the skipper would say, "You're off course," hell no wonder, my hands were practically frozen to the wheel. The only warmth I got was when the engineer brought us both a mug of tea each.

Midnight came and my relief came half an hour late, he had been sea sick. I was wet through to the skin and cold as I came off the bridge. I headed for the boiler top and, being so wet and tired, I flopped down on the steel gratings and fell asleep. It seemed only minutes since I had gone to sleep when I was shook awake by my mate the other deckhand for my turn to go back on watch. I was so warm and dry but on watch I went, still fully clothed. The time was four a.m. so another four hours to be spent on watch. This time the sea had moderated and no spray came over the bow, but then it started raining so we tied a heaving line from the ladders on the funnel to the forward mast, then put a hatch cover over the heaving line to make a rough shelter from the rain. Only trouble was the wind used to get underneath the cover so that meant it felt a lot cooler.

At eight o'clock I was relieved again, back onto the boiler top to sleep and dry off before falling asleep. I was fascinated by the steam rising from my wet gear, it was like being in a mini fog or steam bath. I was only asleep for a couple of hours when I was woken up to get the sea gear in and pull the barges alongside. I looked towards the shore line and noticed a large pier sticking out to sea, it turned out to be Southend-on-Sea pier. Getting the barges hove in and lashed alongside was very hard work, well to us young lads it was.

We were tired, damp and hungry but we pressed on heaving the sea rope in bit by bit until we had the barges lashed alongside of the tug. Then away up to Gravesend and further on. Whilst the skipper and mate were navigating up river we grabbed some breakfast then we started stripping the barges of lamps and batteries. Also I found out we had to take off the barges hatch covers, plus the wooden hatches. Apparently they had to go back to Selby ship builders ready for the next set of barges that were being built.

After delivering the barges up the Thames the next thing was away back home to Hull, it felt good steaming back home. I told the engineer that we had to do fours on the wheel, so now half way through my watch he whistled up to the bridge via the voice pipe and asked if the skipper would let me go down and help dump some ashes from the stokehold.

So, permission granted, I went down the engine room and there was the engineer waiting with two mugs of steaming tea, grinning all over his face, he said "Get that down you." By the way the engineer's name was Jimmy Ryan, he was the son of the Jimmy Ryan who shot the German plane down whilst mate of *Seaman* that I mentioned earlier.

On arrival at Hull we had to go straight to the coal jetty and fill up with bunker coal. Then whilst entering the Alexandra dock the broker shouted "we shall be needing you for the next tide skipper," which turned out to be six o'clock next morning. Us deckhands mumbled to ourselves, we're not coming but we did - all this for £1.50 per week! I must have spent about a year on the *R.W. Wheeldon.*

R. W. Wheeldon
Photo credit Hull Maritime Museum.

Chapter 4
1947 - *Merchantman (1946) [Empire Bess (1946)], Marksman (1914), Englishman (1947) [Enchanter (1945)]*

Merchantman (1946)

After my sixteenth birthday I received orders from our main office for me to join a seagoing tug called the *Merchantman* which was the ex *Empire Bess*. She was moored inside Albert dock in the Town Docks in Hull. She was a lovely looking tug, very clean and what's more she was oil burning and had electric lights. Also the accommodation was on deck level. I never thought a tug could be like this, but only 'cause United Towing had nothing to do with the building of her.

Merchantman (1946)
Photo UTSS collection.

I noticed the deckhands wore nice clean jeans for working in, them days jeans were for working in, not like today, people nowadays wear them for best! So first I purchased new jeans just to be like the other deckhands. *Merchantman* had three deckhands called Gordon Petler, Geoff Howitt plus myself.

Gordon Petler & Geoff Howitt
Photo copyright Gordon Petler.

26

Going back to the accommodation there was room below decks for six runners, this meaning the *Merchantman* could carry extra crew to be transferred to future tows, 'cause most ships that were towed were crewless. However, sailing day came and after getting stores four more crew joined us. Destination was Dakar on the north west coast of North Africa. *Merchantman* was very comfortable after my previous tugs, clean bedding and carpets in every cabin, home from home I thought.

We arrived at Dakar for our tow which was the burnt out shell of a Swedish ship, it was too bad to put runner crew aboard so we towed the vessel with no crew on board. Our destination was Barcelona in Spain. She was to be broken up for scrap. On arrival in Barcelona we were told to stay there and await fresh orders, so a few nights in Spain was sheer luxury because the pound note was worth a fortune in them days. Compared to the Spanish money a glass of beer cost only ten pence in today's money, so you can imagine how far a pound went.

When we eventually got our orders we were delighted because we were contracted out to a French salvage company to tow ex-sunken ships that had been salvaged on the North Africa coast. So we sailed to our first African port of Algiers for oil bunkers.

Funny thing happened whilst we were taking on bunkers, a scraggy looking dog was stood on the quayside, it's bones were sticking out all over, it also had sores on it's body. I felt sorry for it, we gave it food and water but our skipper, called Stewart Nicholson, told us not to let the dog come aboard, which we had no intention of doing.

After the dog had been fed it disappeared along the quay and we thought no more about it, however, we set sail bound for Tobruk where some of the wrecks were ready to be towed away. Whilst on watch during the night we were yarning about the dog we had seen. When the bridge phone went it was the engineer saying "Hell there's a dog asleep on the engine room hatchway", so after speaking to the engineer we decided to keep quiet about the dog until the next day. Next day we reported the dog to the skipper, to our surprise he just smiled and said we had better call him Algee. So the dog became part of the crew, we bathed him and treated his sores, he turned out to be a nice dog.

On arrival in Tobruk we saw dozens of ships that had been bombed and sunk during the Second World War, consisting of British ships, American Liberty ships, some Italian and ex-German ships.

Draco, Tobruk to Cartagena.

One British ship turned out to be a Hull ship of Ellerman's Wilson Line called *Draco*. [5] Now there's no accommodation left aboard so the French salvage company built log cabins on the decks of these wrecks for our runner crew to live in. Drums of water were put aboard plus a portable cooking stove and four days food. The hulls of these wrecks were covered in

---

[5] From Wrecksite.

On 11/04/1941 the Ellerman's Wilson cargo steamer *DRACO* was bombed by aircraft and sunk at Tobruk with the loss of 1 life. The vessel was raised in February 1948 and finally broken up at Valencia on 13/09/1948.

mussels, deck wise of course these were dead but under water these mussels like shell fish were quite alive.

Draco
Photo copyright unknown – Public domain.

We towed our first wreck to Cartagena, a Spanish port, but on arrival the Spanish Harbour Master came aboard to inspect the tow. The crafty Harbour Master said a berth was not ready for the tow until the next day so *Merchantman* anchored with the tow still connected with a short tow rope astern.

Within an hour the Harbour Master's boat had returned towing small boats with fishermen aboard who then started scraping the mussels off the side of the tow's hull. Some skin divers came and went underneath the hull to collect the mussels but our runner crew aboard the tow told us they were kept awake at night by the wind blowing through the dead dried mussels. However, they said they enjoyed the experience, a couple of glorious nights were spent ashore then away back we sailed to Tobruk for our next tow.

On arrival at Tobruk we found out that our next tow was half a liberty ship, the stern half of a ship that had broken in two halves during the war. Same as the last tow when a log cabin had been built on the deck, this time an old life boat was just sat aboard the tow, this was filled with stores and lashed down. There was no way you could launch this boat if the tow sank, they would have had to just sit in it and hope to float off. Unthinkable but that's how it was in the early days after the war. We set off again towing the stern half of the liberty boat only this time we were bound for another Spanish port called Valencia. This time we were allowed straight into the harbour where locals also started stripping the tow of mussels, we used to call these tows the mussel run.

After a nights stay in Valencia we set sail for Tobruk again to tow the bow half of the liberty ship, only this time we were to tow the bow section to Cartagena. The bow half of the liberty ship wasn't quite ready for us so we decided to venture ashore to have a look around. All there was ashore were some sheds for makeshift cafés, inside Arabs sat drinking coffee and smoking hashish, a kind of drug that they smoked. Our skipper told us to be back on board for nine o'clock that evening, if not we would be left ashore and our motor boat would return to the tug without us. Yes, we missed the last boat and true to his word we were left ashore.

During the daytime it gets really hot but the evening is quite cold as we soon found out. We finished up trying to sleep in an old burnt out German tank but some time after midnight we left our tank and walked down to the quay and to our surprise our motor boat had come back for us. We were freezing cold because we only had shorts and thin tee shirts on, the skipper taught us a lesson that night for sure.

Our orders changed, we were to tow the bow half to Barcelona. After connecting the tow we set off again, but during the voyage we heard a clanging sound coming from the tugs propeller area. After handing over the tow at Barcelona, inspection was made to the propeller and it was decided to put *Merchantman* into a floating dry dock which in turn moved across the harbour and put the tug onto some concrete chocks. After placing *Merchantman* on the chocks the dry dock moved away leaving the tug high and dry for repairs to be carried out. It turned out that the damage wasn't done to the propeller it was a piece of metal come loose from the stern post.

The problem now was the floating pontoon dry dock that put Merchantman onto the chocks now had a Spanish vessel inside it for a three week refit, meaning we had to wait three weeks before we could leave our said chocks. Well as you can imagine hell broke loose, but us lads aboard the tug had a whale of a time ashore every night.

Saturdays was bull fighting days, I wasn't keen on seeing the bull fights myself, only went the once.

We did quite a few trips from North Africa to various Spanish ports during our stay in the Mediterranean. Last job we did before returning home was to tow another wreck from Suez, yon side of the Suez Canal. The tow from there was an oil tanker called *Tynefield*, apparently she had been bombed during the war, sunk in the canal but raised later. Only three quarters of the *Tynefield* was left, this we towed through the Suez Canal on to Genoa in Northern Italy. After leaving Genoa we called at Algiers for bunker oil. We had no sooner moored to the quay when our passenger, the now fat little dog called Algee, jumped ashore and disappeared. He must have only come for a holiday, however, he was in better condition than he was when he came aboard.

Merchantman towing *Tynefield*
Photo credit Peter Elsom.

Barjora, Bombay to River Tyne.

After bunkering we proceeded back to Hull. On our arrival we were told that our leave had been cancelled. We had been away six months. The reason was that we had to sail the next day for Bombay in India and had to get there as soon as possible.

So away we went back the way we had come. It took us four weeks to sail to Bombay via the Suez Canal, then Aden and on to Bombay. After all the rush of getting there quick we were told that our tow called *Barjora,* a British Indian Steamship company passenger vessel hadn't arrived. Apparently she was still at sea coming to Bombay in a weeks time.

Whilst waiting in Bombay the decks were covered in Indian traders selling all sorts, including a snake charmer. If he collected enough money he'd set up a fight between a snake and a mongoose. We all put our money together to see this, it was amazing to see a little mongoose kill a large snake, but I thought afterwards just how cruel it really was.

After a few days our tow *Barjora* arrived at Bombay harbour and anchored. After she discharged her passengers and cargo we were told she was all ours for towing back to the UK. The vessel looked in good condition, I'd have thought it would have been easier to steam herself back to the U.K. but, whatever, that's what was wanted by her owners.

They had sold her for scrap, it took *Merchantman* eight weeks to tow the *Barjora* back to the U.K. via Suez again. We finally arrived on the River Tyne and handed her over to local dock tugs and proceeded back to Hull for a fortnights leave.

Barjora
Photo copyright unknown – Public domain.

Moorhen, Trincomalee to Sheerness.

After our leave our new destination was to be back more or less where we had come from, only this time we were going to Ceylon, now called Sri Lanka. We were bound for an ex naval base called Trincomalee. After the war this port was closed and all naval vessels came back to the U.K. Some vessels had to be towed, our tow was to be a lifting craft called *Moorhen*. During our outward passage we were approaching the Red Sea from the Gulf of Suez where there are two very small islands called the Brothers - one had a fixed lighthouse unmanned and the other was the remains of a lighthouse, also the remains of some sort of accommodation. The reason we know is our skipper decided to put our motor lifeboat down and go and have a quick look around, there was a lovely sandy beach running around these little islands. We stepped onto the beach and walked towards the wrecked buildings, I remember it felt really scary. I heard in later years that some Arab sailors had murdered the occupants of the wrecked buildings just for their food stores and equipment but it happened years ago before my time.

We arrived at Trincomalee, the jetties were covered in a lot of growth, the jungle was taking over with monkeys swinging about in the near trees. We never stopped long for we sailed the next day towing the *Moorhen* back to Sheerness, but we nearly became a wreck ourselves. One clear moonlit night as we were in the Indian Ocean approaching the Gulf of Aden I was on the twelve to four watch with the second mate, a nice chap called Les Sumpton, however at two a.m. I came off the bridge to make our tea and toast.

Whilst waiting for the urn to boil I came on deck to talk to engineer Ernie Callan, a good friend of mine, we were both looking out to sea just gazing and yarning when we both heard a sound like waves crashing then we noticed a thin white line, I soon realised it was a beach we were looking at. I rushed back onto the bridge, grabbed the steering wheel off the second mate, put it hard over to port, I then said to the second mate, "Look over your starboard side," poor Les disappeared to get the skipper out, we were running alongside the beach, lucky for us we were still in deep water.

Moorhen
Photo by Barry Dixon. From RFA website.

It turned out that the island we were running alongside of was called Socotra, a narrow escape. If I hadn't gone to make tea things could have been a lot worse indeed. The reason why we nearly came unstuck was the last noon sight was slightly wrong, the island of Socotra had no lights on it and marked on the chart it says keep at least three miles clear of the islands! Also radar in them days was out of the question for most ships never mind tugs, it was then in its early stages, only naval ships had radar to begin with. If we had radar on this occasion we would have seen the islands sooner.

We arrived at Sheerness pretty quickly because the *Moorhen* was only as big as the *Merchantman* so we made quite a good speed.

Corvettes, Montreal to Hamburg.

Next trip, Canada, so now we crossed the Atlantic and made our way to Montreal running loose this time. Our tows were two corvettes, ex-navy escort vessels. We had some hellish weather crossing the Atlantic but arrived okay.

We spent a bit of time in Montreal waiting for good weather reports, also there was reported some small icebergs said to have been seen. These were called growlers, I don't know why. However, we set sail down the Saint Lawrence River only to be told to berth at Quebec. We stayed there for a couple of days, then away to sea. Our destination was Hamburg in Germany.

Both corvettes were in good condition but apparently they were both going to be converted to whale chasers for the Norwegian government. They were delivered to Hamburg okay.

May 1950 – Corvettes, Montreal to Hamburg.
Photo copyright Gordon Petler.

Capt. Billy Hopper

Next voyage was quite interesting also. We had a new captain called Billy Hopper, later to become Marine Superintendent for United Towing.

Captain William Hopper
Photo copyright Pete Bass.

We sailed down to Southampton, our tow was a brand new floating dry dock built for the Brazil government. Also we had brought a runner crew along with us to crew the floating dry dock, for those who have never seen a dry dock, well it's more or less a large type of barge with two walls built either side. One wall served as the accommodation and the other wall was the machine house and pump rooms. To use the dry dock they flooded the barge so that it would sink deep enough for a vessel to float into, then once the vessel was inside the tanks were pumped out and so raised the vessel until dry, more or less like a submarine that goes up and down.

So ahead of us we had about a four thousand mile tow. Our destination was Belem up the River Amazon. We set sail after transferring the runner crew and stores aboard the dry dock. In the Bay of Biscay we ran into some bad weather but the floating dry dock rode out the gales okay. It was strange watching the seas rolling through the dry dock.

The runner crew were okay up on top of the walls, we spoke to them regularly on walkie talkie sets. Every day we blew the tugs steam whistle at noon so they could set their clocks. Between the two walls on the dry dock was rigged a gangway between because the galley and mess room was on one side of the walls whereas sleeping accommodation was on the opposite side. After blowing this whistle at noon it looked quite funny to see the runner crew walk across the gangway to the mess room for lunch, they resembled the seven dwarves when they walked across.

Our new captain, Billy Hopper, was a very strict captain at first. Our crew on board *Merchantman* had all been together for about three years and we were like a family, worked happy together. The last skipper was the free and easy type called Nicholson, this same captain Nicholson smoked a pipe. One day I heard him moaning about having too much pipe tobacco aboard, up till then I had never smoked, so I said to him "If you give me a pipe I'll smoke some for you", well he gave me a pipe and I had my first puff, I nearly choked myself at first but in the end did manage it and continued smoking the pipe and enjoyed it.

After the voyage, on my bond bill was one pipe sold to me for two pounds, hell I thought I had been doing him a favour. However, I continued smoking a pipe for years to come.

Now back to my yarn about Captain Hopper. I was placed on his watch for the first part of the voyage to Belem, South America. Now the last skipper had made us deckhands a stool to sit on whilst steering 'cause he thought standing for four hours caused varicose veins!

For years we enjoyed this privilege, however Captain Hopper was having none of this, so away went the stool to all our disappointment. So standing to attention at the wheel I then put one hand in my pocket and was steering quite well with my other hand. Soon as Captain Hopper saw this his remark was "What's wrong with your other hand, you need two hands to steer properly."

Then come to changing watches. After handing over the wheel to my relief we usually spoke to each other, such as what's for lunch etc., when Captain Hopper heard us talking he said to me "Are you off watch then?" I replied "Oh yes" he said "Well make room for those that are on then," meaning clear off!

A lot of people knew Captain Hopper as a non smoker but I can recall when he smoked one cigarette per day, only one mind you. He always took the four to eight watch in the morning, after taking his star with his sextant early morning I brought him a cup of tea. He would take out a tobacco tin then roll a cigarette, light it, then after two or three puffs threw the half cigarette overboard, and so that was it until the next morning - that tobacco must have lasted the whole trip.

Eventually we entered the mouth of the River Amazon and appearing out of the blue two small gun boats were seen to be catching us up. It turned out that these two gun boats had been built at Southampton and had made the sea passage from Southampton to the Amazon in various stages. We found out that this dry dock we were delivering was for the gun boats.

We finally arrived at Belem and anchored the dry dock. We in turn moored up to the quay and that evening went ashore boozing etc. However, come about ten o'clock we heard gun fire and people dashing in houses. We were told that a curfew was for ten o'clock and if people were found on the streets after ten o'clock they were liable to be shot. So seeing a door inside an alleyway a woman beckoned us in and the door slammed behind us - it turned out to be a brothel. Once inside we noticed small hammocks with very small children asleep inside and pools of wee under each one, it looked revolting to me. We all slept inside a small room with settees to sleep on. As expected some of our lads disappeared (guess where).

Next morning I purchased a baby parrot off the woman and ventured back aboard. After a rollicking from Captain Hopper we sailed back to the U.K. We all took to the baby parrot especially Captain Hopper. He used to play a lot with it as we all did, but sadly on arrival at Hull the customs found the parrot and informed us it was illegal to import parrots. As a compromise it was agreed to kill the poor parrot, but as you can imagine none of the crew would do it. One of the customs men agreed to do it and afterwards the parrot was cremated in the galley stove. We were almost brought to tears, that's the sick parrot story.

Now this story may upset certain people but I was there. It's regarding the *Flying Enterprise* that sank off Lands End. *Merchantman* and *Englishman* had just finished twin towing a vessel to Glasgow when the distress message from *Flying Enterprise* was received saying a crack had appeared fore side of her bridge and she was in danger of flooding. We received orders to steam towards Falmouth, in other words towards *Flying Enterprise*. *Englishman* (Capt. Tim Bond) and *Merchantman* arrived at *Flying Enterprise's* position, no other tugs were there at this time.

Our skippers from *Merchantman* and *Englishman* offered our assistance. Now we had salvage pumps aboard and could have easily transferred these pumps aboard the *Flying Enterprise* but Capt. Carlson of "*Enterprise*" refused our assistance saying his company had a contract for the tug *Turmoil* to assist and tow, trouble was that the *Turmoil* was nowhere to be seen. She was towing some vessel miles away and wouldn't be arriving until the next day. By this time the *Flying Enterprise* was starting to list over slightly but no way would Capt. Carlson let *Englishman* or *Merchantman* anywhere near his vessel.

The next day the tug *Turmoil* arrived on the scene. He came alongside the *Flying Enterprise* with a bang and whilst *Turmoil* bumped heavily onto *Flying Enterprise's* side the mate from the *Turmoil* finished up on board the *Flying Enterprise*. Now whether he fell aboard or stepped aboard is not clear but newspapers and the television described it as a famous leap. We also learned that no way was the *Flying Enterprise* to be towed into a British port. But why?

By now the crew of the *Flying Enterprise* had been taken off just leaving the captain and of course the mate from *Turmoil*. *Merchantman* proceeded to Falmouth to embark television and newspaper reporters and baskets of food for them and steam back to *Flying Enterprise*.

On arriving back we were just in time to witness *Turmoil* trying to make a connection to the *Flying Enterprise*. Now imagine just two men trying to pull a tow wire from *Turmoil* onto *Flying Enterprise*, you could see that the tow wire was very thin indeed and easily pulled aboard, *Turmoil* stretched the tow wire and guess what? - it just parted. No further attempt was made to reconnect, neither would *Flying Enterprise* ask *Englishman* or *Merchantman* to assist. The television people and reporters were as sick as could be so we had to more or less hold them up whilst they took their pictures and made up stories.

Capt. Tim Bond on *Englishman* astern of *Flying Enterprise*.
Photo copyright unknown – Public domain.

As we all know *Flying Enterprise* lay on her side for quite a few hours then Captain Carlsen and the mate of the *Turmoil* abandoned her before she sank. In my opinion she could have been saved. Rumour had it that she was carrying a cargo of something that the American government wanted to keep secret, especially as *Flying Enterprise's* last port was Hamburg in Germany. Much later a salvage ship with divers aboard was seen working on the wreck.

Capt. Hopper takes *Merchantman* close in to *Flying Enterprise*
to give seasick cameramen their final shots before she sinks.
Photo copyright unknown – Public domain.

Promotion to Mate

On arrival back home I left *Merchantman* and joined the docking tugs. I was asked to join a tug called *Marksman* as a mate.

Marksman (1914)
Photo UTSS collection.

I spent a few months aboard the *Marksman* then I transferred to *Englishman*. Back to sea, only this time I was second mate.

Englishman (1947) [Enchanter 1945]
Photo UTSS collection.

Our first job was to Iceland to tow a trawler back to Hull.

As I can remember the trawler's name was *St. Crispin* which had been aground somewhere off Iceland.

H86 St Crispin
Photo UTSS collection.

After delivering the trawler back to Hull our next voyage was to be Canada again, to tow a brand new lake boat from Newcastle to Montreal.

Laker from Newcastle to Montreal.

We set sail towing the lake boat through the Pentland Firth and away towards Canada. Half way, somewhere near the Grand Banks we ran into dense fog with a huge swell. You couldn't see the tow, all you could see was the tow rope disappearing over the stem. What with no radar the only thing we had was a sounding machine, so it was dead reckoning most of the way.

It must have been two am in the morning when the *Englishman* just stopped rolling. It was flat calm very quickly and also blowing the ship's whistle produced an echo. Not liking this I woke the skipper up, Tim Bond, who suspected what I had suspected, that we were steaming alongside an iceberg. So engines reduced to dead slow we plodded on. By eight o'clock we started rolling again and the ships whistle wasn't finding echo again.

By noon the fog had cleared and we were surrounded by Spanish fishermen - biggest wonder was that we hadn't had a collision during the fog. Whilst heaving the tow rope inboard there was several glass fishermen floats wrapped around the tow rope and bits of netting, however, no mishaps had been reported. Sometimes I've seen fishermen go between tugs and tow and get away with it.

After delivering the lake boat at Montreal we were told another job was coming up. We just stayed where we were in Montreal awaiting fresh orders. We had a whale of a time in Montreal. We had a good crew but my special friends were a bosun named 'Pongo' and engineer Syd Hawkins. Well after we had been ashore drinking merry we came back aboard partying it. Now the bosun and engineer and myself formed a skiffle group like Lonnie Donegan, a famous singer of the time. Pongo had a large galley pan which he used to imitate a guitar, I had two large spoons on my knee and Syd had some kind of biscuit tin for a drum. It sounded okay, in fact we used to finish up in the skipper's cabin partying and singing our heads off.

We then received orders to sail to Panama, South America for an overdue boiler clean but some of the crew said they weren't re-signing on for this next voyage. They had spotted the tug's articles that were pinned up in the crew's focsle stating North Atlantic only. However, they stopped aboard until Panama then flew home.

Andrea Doria

On 25th July 1956, whilst on passage to Panama we picked up a distress call from an Italian passenger liner called *Andrea Doria,* saying she's in dense fog and had been in a collision.

Thus given her latitude and longitude position I found we were a hundred and sixty miles south of her location. This, by the way, was three am on the morning watch. I called skipper Tim Bond out of bed and he told me to turn *Englishman* around and proceed towards *Andrea Doria*.

Andrea Doria
Photo copyright unknown – Public domain.

39

We kept trying to call the *Andrea Doria* several times to no avail. We got a signal from the American coast guard stating that the *Andrea Dora* had sunk very quickly after passengers and crew had been transferred onto a Swedish passenger ship called *Stockholm*. It turned out that it was the *Stockholm* that had collided with the *Andrea Doria*. The *Stockholm's* bow was badly damaged but was water tight and she was proceeding slowly towards New York, escorted by the American coast guard vessel.

So *Englishman* resumed course towards Panama. We also learned that it was *Andrea Doria's* maiden voyage!

Stockholm
Photo credit: Loomis Dean/The LIFE picture collection/Getty Images.

We arrived in Panama and spent a few days boiler cleaning. When the boiler was cleaned we received orders to proceed to Peru on the west coast of South America, via the Panama Canal which was very interesting going through, because the ruling was that a local crew boarded the *Englishman* and tended the moorings through the several locks. Also the pilot brought his own helmsman with him so we all more or less laid back and enjoyed the scenery.

Scrap ships, Peru to UK.

Once through the Panama Canal we proceeded to Lima in Peru. On arrival we were introduced to our tow which was an old type of cargo ship but it seemed fully loaded. We soon found out her cargo was the remains of another vessel which had been broken up and dumped inside the one we were to tow back to the U.K.

We painted over her previous name and stencilled B.S.Co. Number 6 onto her bow, 'British Steel Corporation' such was the demand for scrap steel after World War Two. So away we sailed back to the U.K. via the Panama canal again, also via Bermuda for oil bunkers.

HMRT Enchanter
Photo UTSS collection.

I forgot to mention that this *Englishman* was in fact last named *H.M.S. Enchanter,* United Towing bought her after the war and renamed her *Englishman* replacing the other *Englishman* that was lost during the war. I left *Englishman* and rejoined the river tugs as a mate aboard several tugs, eventually becoming Master of the river and coastal tug called *Norman.*

Charlie's first command, 1957-60. Steam Tug *Norman.*
Charlie on the bridge towing BI ship *Chupra* towards King George Dock lock, Hull.
Photo UTSS collection.

Chapter 5
1960's - *Norman (1929), Foreman (1959), Masterman (1964), Tradesman (1964)*

Fleet modernisation.

I spent three years aboard of the tug *Norman*, then transferred to a coastal tug called *Foreman* which was pretty new. In fact she was the first tug that United Towing had built since before the war. Below decks she was comfortable enough but on deck mostly not. She had an open bridge, the same as the old tugs, and we did quite a lot of coastal and continental work in her. I spent almost two and a half years aboard the *Foreman*.

Foreman (1959), on sea trials.
Photo UTSS collection.

One day in 1960 our chairman and owner Mr. Spink died at his desk at the grand old age of eighty five. Apparently now United Towing was up for sale and we had no idea what was going to happen. However, all the tug skippers were requested to come to our main office to meet our new owner who turned out to be a trawler owner by the name of Sir Basil Parks.

He was very interesting to listen to, he explained that he intended to modernise the tug fleet and also that he was going to put radar on some of the tugs. He explained that the old steam sea going tugs were for sale, they weren't making a profit as there was strong competition from the continent, mainly the Dutch. So one by one over a period of time the large sea going tugs were sold. Then some of the old docking tugs were converted to diesel tugs and our working hours were reduced. We started to get every other weekend off and we worked on a Sunday, especially tugs that had to do standby turns. On a Sunday we got double time, something that was never heard of with the United Towing old bosses.

As promised new tugs were being built. First were two twin screw coastal come river tugs called *Headman* and *Workman*, then later three more slightly larger tugs were built called *Tradesman*, *Merchantman*, and *Masterman*, all two thousand horse power each. I was informed by our new Superintendent, Captain Garrod that I was going to be taking command of the new *Masterman* when she was completed.

I was invited to the launching of the *Merchantman* at Hessle shipyard where the new tugs were being built. I was also introduced to our new Managing Director, a Mr. Wilbraham, a nephew of Sir Basil Parks - a nice polite chap I thought.

Then came the launching ceremony. *Merchantman* was being launched sideways and some lady who launched the tug let fly with the champagne bottle, but instead of landing onto the tug's bow it flew over the bow and landed amongst some onlookers.

Another bottle was quickly found and this time the bottle hit the bow and away *Merchantman* went sideways into the River Hull. During a few speeches it was said that the bottle incident wasn't unlucky but sadly, a few years on, *Merchantman* did sink, but that's another story.

Merchantman (1964)
Photo UTSS collection.

Masterman (1964)

After taking command of *Masterman* we were involved in river and continent work mostly berthing large tankers onto Saltend oil jetty and Killingholme jetty south of the Humber.

Now on the south bank of the Humber are the docks at Immingham, then owned by the railway company. It was only used by mine sweepers during the war years and there was only two tugs working there and these tugs were the property of the railway company, known as Railway Tugs.

The only trouble was that they only worked nine to five each day and if any vessel came to Immingham during the night then we put them onto the jetty and left them there to await nine o'clock for the Railway Tugs to berth them. We wasn't allowed to enter Immingham dock to berth ships. Things changed though, a small tug firm called Piggots of Grimsby fought in court for the right to be allowed to berth ships at Immingham dock.

The story goes that Piggots owners in Grimsby put every penny they had to fight their case to be allowed to work in Immingham docks with their tugs and successfully won their case. So now Piggots were looking for some larger tugs because they only had small tugs berthed at Grimsby. They purchased some second hand tugs from London. These old tugs were stable and were purchased from Sun Towage Company of London. In fact one of United Towing tugs finished up working for Piggots. It was the ex *Brahman*, later called *Lady Vera*.

Brahman (1938)
Photo UTSS collection.

Lady Vera (1962) [Brahman 1938]
Photo UTSS collection.

In the meantime United Towing's new owners had started building new sea going tugs because it was whispered that gas and oil may be found in the North Sea. Survey vessels were sounding for oil and gas so the North Sea was divided into sections between every country bordering the North Sea.

The first large sea tug that was built was called *Englishman* again, this was some time in the sixties. One day on *Englishman's* maiden voyage, and along with *Serviceman* and myself in *Masterman* we set sail for Middlesbrough to tow an oil rig out to a position twenty miles east of the Humber. I remember that *Englishman* and *Serviceman* were to tow the drilling rig and I was to escort with a television crew aboard. Trouble was the oil drilling rig was a very large barge converted to drill complete with a drilling tower.

The barge had six long legs [10], three [5] either side, the idea was that once on location these legs were lowered down to the sea bed then hydraulic jacks jacked up the barge clear of the water, because proper oil rigs were in the future if any oil or gas was discovered.

After waiting for suitable weather we all set off from Middlesbrough with high hopes of finding oil or gas. The location for the oil rig was marked off with red plastic buoys in two lines and in the centre was placed a green plastic buoy. The green buoy was the marker for the drilling tower to be placed over. About three miles from location our big brand new tug *Englishman* developed engine trouble. So now I had to tow *Englishman* clear to anchor then take her place towing the oil rig into position. Looking back I think the oil platform was named *Sea Gem*.

Sea Gem leaving Middlesborough under tow of
Englishman & *Serviceman*, assisted by *Masterman.*
Photo taken from *Masterman,* copyright Fred Fletcher.

We slowly towed the platform toward the green buoy and as soon as it was in position there was a very large crashing sound. Turned out that the legs on the platform were released and thundered down to the sea bed, then very slowly the platform was raised and tugs were released.

The TV crew that were aboard the Masterman got some really good shots that day. They made a documentary for BBC1 called North Sea Gamble - let's face it it was a gamble in those days.

There was a lot more to come. The Americans were very much involved. In Rotterdam an old British tanker was being converted. On its focsle head was built a very large crane, its jib just reached fore side of the bridge and it had a thousand ton lift.

Then six anchors on special winches - one lead out forward, one each side of the bows, one straight out astern and one out of each quarter. These anchors were attached with long wires to the ring of the anchors and on the crown of the anchors another wire with a large buoy attached. Now this was where *Masterman* and *Merchantman* came in. Our bows were fitted with large rollers and were now contracted out to this converted tanker called *Global Adventurer,* American owned but with a Dutch crew. Now if gas and oil were discovered then *Global Adventurer* would cover the ex-drilling area with a large platform using its large crane. But *Masterman* first had to place these anchors out from *Global Adventurer.*

First the large crane would swing these anchors overboard one by one, first the head or forward anchor, then *Masterman's* job was to pick up these anchors, winch them aboard. The wire attached to each buoy came through a special drilled out hole in the buoy. Once we had heaved the anchor off the bottom we were then given a course to steer, full speed to keep the anchor wire as taut as possible, then when the anchor was stretched far enough out we were told to let go of the anchor, and anchor now on the sea bed. We came back to *Global Adventurer* to repeat the same performance with the other anchors so *Global Adventurer* was set up on six anchors. Then came tugs towing huge barges and on the barges deck welded down was a large platform. This barge was towed alongside *Global Adventurer* and moored up, then this large crane shackled onto the platform taking the slack up. Then dozens of Spanish workers with burning gear set to cutting the welding that was securing the platform to the barge and so the platform was raised up onto *Global Adventurer's* deck to prepare it for lowering onto the found gas area where it was pile driven to the sea bed.

When recovering *Global Adventurer's* anchors mostly in bad weather it was very dangerous. Mainly when fetching the large crane to lift the anchors back aboard from the tug the block on the crane had a hook on the end, our crew had to hook the anchor wire onto it - this being done whilst *Masterman* was rolling about, so was this large hook! We continued with this type of working with *Global Adventurer* for about six weeks then "*Global*" sailed back to Rotterdam and we made our way back to Hull.

Global Adventurer
Photo copyright Fred Fletcher.

Later we heard from our office that we might be assisting the *Sea Gem* platform off the Humber, which we had placed earlier, to move only a matter of a few feet. Sounded simple enough, just heave its legs up then re-drop them again but I'm afraid it wasn't to be. Apparently the day before it was due to be moved they had decided to lower the platform for a quicker lower when the tugs were due next day.

Masterman was twelve hours from this location and making our way there to assist then disaster struck. Whilst they were lowering the legs on the platform the hydraulics on one side of the barge collapsed, so three [5] legs gone on one side of the barge and the other three [5] on the other side still standing, it had to happen. The whole rig turned turtle, drowning many of its crew. When we arrived in *Masterman* all that you could see was a single leg sticking out of the sea bed and gas bubbling to the surface. [6]

We were then ordered to station ourselves there to warn off any shipping that might come near. After a few days we were relieved and made our way back to Hull.

My crew, on arrival, said "When you go to the office tell them that if we are required to go back to *Global Adventurer* to do some anchor handling then we need extra pay." (We used to call it anchor snatching). If not they would not go back. I must admit it was dangerous work. I mentioned this to the office, they informed the American owners of *Global Adventurer* and straight away they said "Give them what they want, we need them again." So myself and crew finished up with double pay next time we was to work *Global Adventurer.*

Anchor handling in the 60's, from the bow.
Johnny Handley (outboard), George Hatch (above), & Tony Iveson.
Off Cabinda with *Global Adventurer.* Note UTC regulation safety boots!
Photo copyright Peter Elsom.

[6] From Wrecksite.

Then, on 27-12-1965, disaster struck. As the 32-man crew was lowering Sea Gem so that it could be towed to a new site, two of its ten legs suddenly collapsed and the platform sank, leaving five men dead and eight others missing. With it, Britain's hopes for a quick commercialization of the North Sea gas reserves received a setback.

1966 - Cheating Death.

Now this next story is about when I nearly lost my life. One of the platforms that *Global Adventurer* had positioned off Yarmouth early in the year had been damaged by some ship colliding with it. This platform had to be lifted and repaired. *Masterman* ran "*Global's*" anchors out, "*Global*" started to repair the damaged platform, then bad weather set in. The forecast had predicted bad weather for at least a week, so the powers that be decided to lift the platform onto *Global Adventurer's* deck. *Masterman* recovered her anchors then we all proceeded to the River Humber.

On arrival in the Humber "*Global*" wanted anchors spreading, only this time to moor across the tide. Meaning that the two anchors from the port bow and port quarter took most of the strain during ebb tide and the starboard anchors on flood tide. The head anchor and stern anchor never took much of the strain. When questioned about this it was explained that they intended putting the platform over the side onto the river bed on the lee side so the welders would be sheltered from a westerly wind. Over side went the platform close to "*Global's*" ships side and work began. There was just enough room for *Masterman* to moor alongside the *Global Adventurer's* starboard side.

Now I had been stuck on *Masterman's* bridge for eighteen hours and was very tired so when things had settled down I took a shower, put clean pyjamas on, then with watches set, crashed into my bunk for a well earned sleep, I was knackered. I could hear the burners and welders banging and crashing about, the odd welding rod dropping onto the tugs deck. After a while I fell fast asleep.

About two am in the morning I awoke to the sound of yelling and banging on my door. Apparently the *Global Adventurer* as I predicted had started dragging her anchors, thus drifting onto the platform which Spanish welders were working on and causing a lot of panic. By this time I was on the *Masterman's* bridge and with engines running started to push the *Global Adventurer* away from the platform but I wasn't having much success. Maybe we were just holding our own pressure by pushing, I don't really know because somehow the roller that was attached to *Masterman's* bow became jammed between *Global Adventure's* side and also the platform side.

Whilst I manoeuvred to try and free *Masterman's* bow, *Masterman* started to slowly lay over to port. The welders aboard of the platform were scrambling back aboard *Global Adventurer. Masterman* started listing further to port, I could not go astern to free myself and the list was becoming dangerous. Whilst *Masterman's* bows were still pressed up against "*Global's*" side I ordered my crew to climb aboard the *Global Adventure's* side. By this time a rope ladder had been rigged and lowered to take the crew safely off. I was having a quick look round, I suddenly remembered that the accommodation doors were open. I thought to myself if I'm quick I may have time to dash down and close these doors, which I did. First the accommodation door then I had just managed to screw down the engine room door. By then water was up to my knees. I was about to make my way back to the bridge when suddenly the *Masterman* rolled over onto her port side thus trapping me underwater. That's when I thought I was about to drown, which I nearly did. However, somehow I surfaced quite a good way from the now laid over *Masterman*.

What a way to die I thought - I was still in my pyjamas, bare feet and what's more it was November time. I tried to swim ashore, I could now and again see shore lights but with the strong ebb tide and pitch black night I just drifted on my back slowly freezing.

I could now and again see boats dashing about, probably looking for me. Then I just closed my eyes and waited for the end, strange as it may seem I felt very relaxed, eyes closed. I opened my eyes quickly to the glare of a searchlight. I'd been found by a tug called *Headman* which lucky enough had been working in the river that night. Also whilst most rescue vessels had been searching near the *Global Adventure's* position, *Headman* had gone down river with the tide and I drifted down towards *Headman*.

The Captain of the *Headman* was Stan Cook, one of United Towing's most experienced skippers and his quick reaction going down river saved my life. I was hauled aboard *Headman* and taken to Immingham Dock jetty, boarded an ambulance and away to Grimsby hospital. I was like a block of ice and kept being sick, coughing up salt river water.

I spent a day and a half in hospital then an agent picked me up in a borrowed dressing gown and took me to a tailors shop, and rigged with new clothes I was beginning to feel myself again. They asked if I wanted some money, I accepted ten pounds to buy a new pipe and pipe tobacco. I was driven by car to New Holland then I walked into United Towing's office to report. I was told to take a few days off, but for my own sake I wanted to go straight back on board *Masterman*, which had not sunk or been damaged. She had laid on her side until the flood tide, then she righted herself as the tide changed.

When she became upright the crew had returned back on board and the mate, Ken Bishoprick, brought her back to Hull for examination, They found her to be sound apart from a few scratches to the paintwork.

I returned back on board *Masterman* and completed the contract.

End of the months pay packet I saw that ten pounds had been stopped. I asked what was it for. I was politely told that I had been given the ten pounds in Grimsby after *Masterman's* accident - such was United in those days!

Masterman (1964)
Photo UTSS collection.

1967 *Tradesman (1964)*

Next voyage was seven months long. This time I joined the tug *Tradesman.* We first sailed to Rotterdam to tow a large barge full of small platforms and steel piles for piling the platforms to the sea bed, and much more equipment all neatly welded down for a voyage to Cabinda, Portuguese Africa as it was in them days before independence.

Our first port of call for bunkers was Las Palmas, then onto Cabinda. After arriving at Cabinda we were told to anchor with the barge to await the arrival of *Global Adventurer* which had been to America doing work there.

The day came when *Global Adventurer* arrived. Scattered all over a wide area of the sea were large tubes that turned out to be oil wells freshly drilled. *Global Adventurer's* job was to place these small jackets over the wells to protect them, so work began.

Tradesman (1964)
Photo copyright Graeme Turner.

First we had to anchor our barge, then go and spread *Global Adventurer's* six anchors, then after that bring the barge alongside. They unloaded some of the small platforms and piles onto her decks after which we re-anchored the barge, then "*Global's*" large crane lifted these platforms over the oil wells and pile drove them into the sea bed. That's what we mainly did for seven long months. I say long because we never left the *Tradesman.* Our fuel and stores we took from the *Global Adventurer.*

We were black as hell with the sun but blacker still was our cook, a great guy called Nick who was born in Jamaica. He kept us well fed and entertained, he was a good singer too.

After all the oil wells had been covered a pipe line was rigged between each oil well on the sea bed. How it was done was *Global Adventurer* anchored in a said position and welded sections of pipe together and it was our job to tow these welded sections from the "*Global.*"

They would weld a section together then say to me pull slowly. When a section was overboard the order came to stop, and so this went on for days. There was only me aboard to do this, so speaking to a Yank who was in charge I said "Hell I'm tired out, 'cause I need to sleep, I'm not a robot," he then replied "How much sleep do you need?" I said "At least six or seven hours." He then said "Take four hours rest and sleep fast because we've got to keep moving."

Pipe line completed we was asked to go alongside of *"Global"* to collect some diving gear which was placed aboard *Tradesman's* fore deck, it was a compressor. I was then asked if I had ever done any 'live boating' I thought what the hell does he mean, I soon found out.

What I was asked to do was, a diver would jump off our bow with an air pipe attached from him to the compressor on *Tradesman's* bow, then he was to walk along the sea bed inspecting the pipe line whilst I followed his bubbles with *Tradesman*. They told me it was a regular thing in American tugs, so away we went following the diver's bubbles. I must admit I didn't like the idea but it worked out okay.

After seven long months the contract finished. *Global Adventurer* returned to Rotterdam and we were left to tow the empty barge back to Rotterdam and then back home for a spot o' leave.

We spent happy and rough times working with *Global Adventurer,* both her crew and our crew got on well together, especially *"Global's"* Captain called Bert Frauwen. I often wondered what happened to him because soon after *Global Adventurer* returned to Rotterdam I heard that she was scrapped.

Global Adventurer
Photo copyright unknown – Public domain.

Chapter 6
1970 - *Englishman (1965)*

After our leave finished I was asked to join the *Englishman* which was now stationed at Singapore. I was to relieve Capt. Arthur King, he had been aboard seven months and was pleased to see us.

Our tow was already waiting for us. It was a Japanese tanker going to Japan for repairs. So next day we set off, Enoshima was our destination, via Tokyo. We had a smooth passage to Japan and spent a few days for repairs to our winch which was damaged whilst recovering our sea gear. Then it was back to Singapore for salvage station and to await fresh orders.

Singapore is a lovely place, in fact one of the cleanest places I've been to. Hard to think what went on during the war. However our next assignment was something altogether different. We were off to a war zone, meaning Vietnam.

We were told to sail nowhere and receive orders by code once we were at sea. Apparently an American cargo ship had grounded in the Mekong Delta in the south of Vietnam. Now we knew that a salvage was going on over there so what we were expecting was anybody's guess. After about forty eight hours and approaching Vietnam it was evening. There were American warships scattered all about the area.

The sky was lit up with flares, also the sounds of gun fire. There were no light buoys of any kind for navigation purposes and we never had a chart for inland waters so I decided to anchor for the night. Come next morning a launch came alongside and after instructions we followed the launch to the spot where the vessel was aground.

On arrival we found her name was *Seatrain Washington* of New York. She was heavily loaded deck wise with such as lorries, jeeps and some aircraft. We established what time high tide was and made connection to *Seatrain Washington's* stem with the help of a small tug that ferried our messenger line aboard. Then just before high water we commenced towing, but *Seatrain Washington* was hard and fast.

Seatrain Washington aground in the Mekong Delta, Vietnam.
Photo taken from *Englishman,* copyright Pete Hemmerman.

Whilst this was happening the Americans were continuously shooting into the surrounding bank side. We spent three days trying to free *Seatrain Washington* then luck was with us.

Heavy rain fell during the fourth day, thus causing lots of water to flow down river, and with this extra water the *Seatrain Washington* was re-floated and we towed her to a safe anchorage. We stayed in the area whilst an inspection was carried out but the vessel was sound. She had only been aground on soft mud, so back to Singapore we went.

We were anchored at Singapore for about four weeks then got a call out to some ship which was a hundred miles away, so we got under way full speed. Also a Dutch tug steamed past. Now I knew that this particular tug was not as fast as "Englishman" but very soon found out the reason why. We was only making eight knots when we should have been making twelve knots. Our engineer kept asking me to reduce speed because his engine temperatures were sky high, so I decided to return to Singapore thinking maybe something was fouling the propeller.

On arrival divers inspected the propellers and the hull of the *Englishman* and found nothing. Divers reported though that heavy growth and mussels were on the bronze propellers and suggested we have them cleaned. I informed United Towing of the situation - first I got a rollicking for returning back to Singapore then they finally agreed to have the *Englishman's* bottom scraped clean by a gang of divers. Afterwards we went on speed trials and sure enough, back to twelve knots again.

Bottom scrape – Englishman in Singapore, October 1971
Photo UTSS collection.

It wasn't long before we got orders to proceed to the Seychelles Islands in the Indian Ocean. So away we went and left Singapore for a smooth crossing to the Seychelles, and thankfully twelve knots still!

We arrived at the beautiful islands where long white sandy beaches greeted us. We entered the harbour with pilot on board who explained the reason for us being there. There was an American vessel anchored inside the harbour which we were to tow to Formosa, or Taiwan as it's now called.

The American ship was called *Salesbury.* She had been trading between the United States and India with grain. However the story goes that while inside the Seychelles she had some repairs to do aboard and also the crew wanted paying because they hadn't been paid for weeks. It was also said that the crew went ashore and played havoc with the locals night after night. The *Salesbury* could not obtain spares or stores because nobody could find out who really owned her.

The firm that was supposed to own her turned out to be a barbers shop in New York, so eventually an American naval vessel entered Seychelles, arrested the whole crew and sailed away with them on board. So the *Salesbury* lay in the Seychelles for months, then the local government sold her for scrap, so that's how the *Englishman* became involved.

We sailed one early morning for Taiwan, the weather was good but I was feeling very ill. Sometimes I could hardly make it onto the bridge, short of breath and with a tight chest but I still had to grin and bear it. I suppose the good news was that instead of sailing to Taiwan orders were changed and now the destination was to be Singapore.

On arrival at Singapore we let go of *Salesbury* and handed her over to local river tugs. We then got orders to remain at Singapore on salvage station, but after anchoring *Englishman* I became very ill. I could hardly talk, a doctor came aboard and straight away I went to hospital. The name of the hospital was Glen Eagles. They pumped my lungs out and kept me in for six weeks.

It was also getting towards Christmas. Christmas day came and I was laid there feeling sorry for myself. I remember a vicar, a man of the cloth, saying "Are you well?" in a sing song sort of voice. He was British, but before I could answer him he had moved on. Later that day a Danish padre stopped by my bed with family, his wife and three children, we had a good conversation. Then they gave a present, this being a leather wallet, then they all sang a carol entitled "Oh Holy Night," I've liked that carol ever since. I was choked as you can imagine.

Then came the day I was discharged and back aboard *Englishman* for my gear. Then I was flown home, we had been away for five months.

Chapter 7
1971 - *Statesman (1969) [Alice L. Moran (1966)]*

After my leave I was informed that I would be flying out to South Africa, Durban to join the tug *Statesman* to relieve Captain Jack Golden. *Statesman* was the ex *Alice L. Moran,* an American tug that United Towing had purchased. She was a large ocean tug with ten thousand horse power, twin screw and a crew of twenty-two, including two wireless operators. The chief wireless operator was Keith Appleyard, a very keen operator at his job which he proved later on in the voyage.

After settling down we spent most of the time moored in Durban. My first mate was Fred Fletcher, a powerful strong lad he was. We used to sit yarning about most things regarding tugs etc. every night in my cabin. You never had much crew trouble whilst Fred was around.

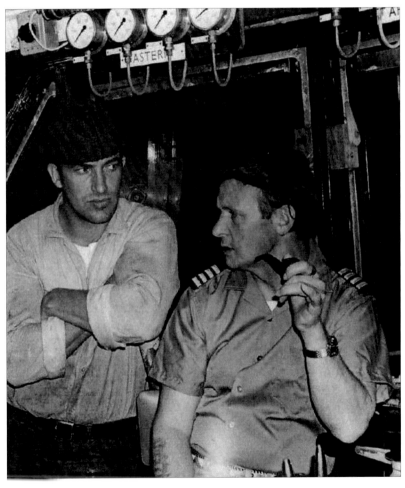

Fred Fletcher and Charlie Noble on the bridge of *Statesman*
Photo copyright The Argus.

One tea time I heard a lot of shouting and yelling coming from the galley, next minute up came the cook complaining that a crew member, Judd was laid on his back inside the galley shouting "Feed me," he was as drunk as hell. I went down and politely said to him "Are you going to move yourself then?" he replied with a big loud "No." So losing my temper I spotted a large gash bin just outside the galley. You name it, it was in there, so I gave him one more chance. He said "No" again so he got the lot, I emptied the whole gash bin over his head. That moved him quick enough.

Things getting a bit boring we used to just walk to the Seaman's mission and back. One night we had just arrived back on board and was thinking of having an early night when the agent came aboard and told us we had to sail immediately to Cape Town. So crew aboard we made our way round to Cape Town.

On arrival at Cape Town it was explained to me that an oil tanker called *Alkis* was anchored off Tristan de Cunha, a small island in the South Atlantic. It was reported that she had a crack midships and that her crew of Greeks refused to sail any further in her. So *Statesman* embarked salvage association officials, plus United Towing's own salvage officer (Capt. Tony Oakley), plus a load of steel girders along with shipyard burners and welders. We were also carrying three reporters from the local newspapers at Cape Town.

Fully loaded away we sailed for Tristan de Cunha. I remember we had bad weather most of the way, the poor reporters were sea sick. They asked me if we could turn back to Cape Town with them, this was halfway across the Atlantic. I said "No way, you were determined to come so grin and bear it."

It was the first time United Towing had allowed reporters aboard their vessels. The cook was moaning and groaning about him having to cook for all these extra passengers. When I told him that he would be paid extra money that soon cheered him up. So onward we went.

July 1971 Cape Town reporters off Tristan de Cunha.
L to R, Bill Goddard (Argus), Louis Blom (Die Burger) and Hugh Murray (Cape Times)
Photo copyright The Argus.

On our arrival at Tristan de Cunha we moored alongside of the *Alkis* and made our inspection of the supposed crack on the *Alkis's* deck. You would need a magnifying glass to see it. So whilst the salvage association officials were making their inspections we lowered our motor boat and went ashore. I did not want to tell folks back home that I'd been to Tristan de Cunha and not stepped ashore, that's what you really had to do.

Alkis off Tristan Da Cunha.
Photo copyright The Argus.

There was no beach, no jetties, everything just rock. All they had was a hollowed platform cut out of the rock face with a small crane for lifting their fishing boats up and down because their main income was from catching crawfish and lobsters which they froze.

Now once a month a vessel from South Africa used to bring stores and mail and then return with a cargo of crawfish and lobsters. They called the vessel *R.S.A. Cape Town*. However at this time only a hundred people were left on the island, the majority of the islands population had left after a volcano erupted a few years earlier.

All the population turned out to greet us, it was just like going back in time. They wore Victorian long clothes. I noticed outside some houses a few spinning wheels because they made their own clothes from the sheep that roamed all over the island. There was a little church and a small hut called the post office. Apparently they used to frank stamps for passing ships when they came close for a look see!

One special building housed a jail and a rack full of different hats. Sat inside was a Mister Black. Now Mister Black could be a policeman, a ship pilot, a fireman and the mayor. Also home guard – there was first world war rifles hung up, so he was also defence, all he had to do was to change hats.

Back on board the crew of the *Alkis* still refused to sail after being told that it was safe to do so. By this time the weather started to worsen so I came off the *Alkis* because we were bumping heavily alongside. *Alkis* hove up her anchor because she was dragging towards the islands, so for now it was a stalemate. Nobody was going anywhere fast, just hove to sheltering on the other side of the island, this went on for a couple of days.

The *Alkis* radioed *Statesman* saying that she was in danger of sinking. Apart from a full cargo of crude oil they said that the ballast tanks were full. Also the pump room was flooded and they asked to be taken off. There was a full gale blowing at the time so I told them to give me a lee side and I would attempt to take them off. So this I did with slight damage to myself.

There was a Greek woman amongst the crew and she was one of the last to leave because she was too scared to jump. However my mate Fred Fletcher jumped aboard *Alkis* and more or less threw her aboard of *Statesman*.

Abandon ship – *Alkis* crew transfering to *Statesman*.
Mrs Angela Fousfouka, wife of *Alkis's* Chief Officer contemplates
her fate, nervous and unwilling to jump across.
Photo copyright The Argus.

Statesman alongside *Alkis* to take off the crew.
Charlie can just be seen on the bridge wing.
Photo copyright The Argus.

Now this left *Alkis* drifting close to Tristan de Cunha, something had to be done and quick. I managed to put Fred Fletcher my mate back on board. I told him to slack away a length of anchor cable out then brake hard on, then I recovered Fred Fletcher back on board the *Statesman*.

Now by this time the locals were worried about *Alkis* sinking and ruining their lobster and crawfish industry. I then put my ideas into practice. I put *Statesman's* stern close towards *Alkis's* bow, the crew then passed a rope messenger around *Alkis's* anchor chain then heaved a towing wire around via the rope messenger, then shackled it to its own part. This was being done during the gale, my crew worked very well indeed. We then started towing the *Alkis* out to sea in the direction of Cape Town and to the relief of Tristan de Cunha's fishermen, I do believe they were glad to see the back of *Alkis*.

I was relieved on the bridge to go down to my cabin but on entering my cabin found all the *Alkis's* crew sat around clicking their so called worry beads - I very politely told them where to go!

I was hoping if the weather got any better to put pumps aboard but in gale force conditions it was just impossible. So all we could do was to get *Alkis* as far away from Tristan de Cunha as fast as we could.

Inspection of *Alkis* mid tow.
Photo copyright The Argus.

We were making a good speed, we managed seven knots, and also managed to get eight hundred miles away from the islands. With us pitching and rolling about I could not see the *Alkis's* draft to see if she was sinking further down at all.

I had the eight to twelve watch and this particular night I decided to just lay on top of my bunk after coming off watch. I felt uneasy somehow. I told the mate to keep me informed of any change, then at about two a.m. I was awoke by an A.B. saying I was wanted on the bridge and that *Statesman* wasn't steering properly. I rushed onto the bridge, it was raining very hard so our searchlight could not focus very well but I knew then more or less what the problem was.

The heavy rain cleared and the searchlight picked up the *Alkis's* bow sticking almost upright. Her stern was completely underwater, I would say about seventy feet was sticking out skywards. I immediately instructed our engineers to release the brakes on the towing winch as we were now being pulled astern pretty fast.

The winch wire was now streaming out very fast indeed, smoke was coming from the winch. Then to our relief the tow wire's end flew overboard.

Come daylight it was found that *Alkis's* bow was still sticking out of the water, only this time it was only about ten feet. This ten feet remained sticking up for twenty four hours, then with a loud gush of air she plunged to her grave, leaving behind tons of floating crude oil. Our decks were covered in the stuff, plus there were lots of albatross, dead and struggling to survive.

When I look back at what it would have done to Tristan de Cunha's fishing industry it's hardly worth thinking about.

Nothing for it now but to return back to Cape Town with our cargo of Greek seamen, shipyard workers, and salvage association reps. None too pleased.

On arrival at Cape Town we started to clean *Statesman* up as best as we could and have some repairs done to our bow which had been damaged whilst picking up *Alkis's* crew. We also had to replace our tow wire which was being flown out from the UK.

We were engaged on a daily rate whilst dealing with *Alkis* so it wasn't too bad for United Towing in the long run. The newspaper reporters that we had for the voyage gave us good write-ups in the local newspapers.

Stricken tanker Alkis sinks

From Staff Reporter Bill Goddard aboard the Statesman

THE ALKIS HAS SUNK. After an epic three-week battle to save the 18 567-ton tanker she finally slipped beneath the dark grey Atlantic rollers 650 miles east north-east of Tristan da Cunha at 4 am SA time today.

The final chapter of the desperate saga of the 17-year-old Liberian vessel began at 2.45 am today when Statesman released the tow line connecting the two vessels.

Within 10 minutes only about 12 metres of the tanker's stern was visible above the water.

We watched the eerie climax in the brilliant floodlights of our tug.

After an all-night vigil the stricken ship, which with its cargo is valued at 400 000 dollars (R280 000), sank; leaving only an oil slick and her name-board floating on the surface at daybreak.

The moment the tow-line was released Statesman sent out an all-ship navigational warning.

The tug is expected back in Cape Town on Monday and Alkis officers and the ship's owner will be in the city to arrange repatriation and settle an alleged wage

RELIEF

The sinking of the damaged tanker far from South Africa's coastline will come as a relief to port and other Government authorities who were concerned about the possibility of large-scale pollution if she had broken up or leaked large quantities of her cargo in their areas of control.

It seems unlikely that any serious pollution will result from the vessel having gone down in the position reported.

STATESMAN. — Cape Town, Aug. 3.—
Salvage tug Statesman: Surveyor reports moderate to heavy ranging damage starboard side to bridge wing. forecastle bulwark, aft catwalk and shell plating and port side heavy damage to shell plating. Foregoing attributed to ranging with motor tanker ALKIS off Tristan da Cunha. Damage to starboard lifeboat attributed to heavy weather on passage to and from Tristan da Cunha. Statesman also claiming damage and loss to towing lines and fittings. Tenders for permanent repairs at Cape Town opening tomorrow—Lloyd's Agents per Salvage Association. (See issues of July 28 and 31.)

Report of damage to *Statesman*. 3rd August 1971
Copyright Lloyds List.

Final newspaper report.
Copyright The Argus.

Translation of an article by Louis Blom in the Afrikanse newspaper Die Burger.

Attempted Salvage of S/S ALKIS July 1971

Tough Tuggies
Ken Geen Vries (Know No Fear)

With the increase of shipping around the South African coast the presence of salvage tugs is now a common sight in our harbours. Whilst South Africa has no salvage tugs of its own there are a number of foreign tugs operating from our harbours. What are the seamen like who crew these salvage tugs! Ordinary seamen? Or are they a group of seamen apart?

After a voyage on the *Statesman* that lasted twenty days, a person realises that they are a breed of their own. To begin with, they don't know the word 'fear.' This word is used frequently and often unnecessarily - but in the case of the crew of *Statesman* it is entirely apt. From a young age they go to sea and their work is such a nature that when on a salvage job their lives are continually in danger. The life on board is not easy. Why do these men go to sea? To answer this question a person must watch these men closely. The men who were involved when *Statesman* sailed for Tristan de Cunha in an attempt to salvage the Liberian tanker *Alkis*. For the first time in the company's long history journalists were allowed to make the voyage; for those who went it proved to be an experience not to be easily forgotten. The crew members of *Statesman* are all from Hull, on the banks of the River Humber. It has been traditional that young men of Hull are drawn to tugs, grandfather and fathers all work together. They begin to work very young on tugs. On the *Statesman* they have a fifteen year old, he still works in the galley but it won't be long before he graduates to the danger of the aft deck.

Fred Fletcher a big strong, chief mate of the *Statesman* is a man of the old school and is proud to be mate of the *Statesman* he related with a large smile brightening his open seaman's face, his tug is his pride and his life. When the tow wire, a steel cable of 20cm circumference had linked to the anchor chain of the *Alkis* in a dangerous operation in storm conditions, it was Fred Fletcher who did the job with his bare hands along with the tugs deck crew. The deck crew of the *Statesman* is never older than 25 years, the reason? Experience shows that ones reactions after this age become too slow, a slow reaction can mean the loss of a workmate or severe injuries.

A tough bunch of men these are. Now with one of the best skippers I have come across is Captain Charles Noble who knows his work. He is a man who also started work with the company as a youngster.

He has done all the jobs aboard up to his appointment as master. This man handles *Statesman* masterfully. When the crew of the *Alkis* had to be rescued, Capt. Noble brought his tug alongside the doomed tanker. Many other ships would have been mangled by the giant tanker but in this man's hands the dangerous operation was achieved with minimal damage. Just to watch him manoeuvre was sufficient to reassure us and this trust was really necessary when *Alkis* sank. We watched the death throes of *Alkis*. Capt. Noble said "We don't lose many ships, We don't like it."

Antonia Xilas

After completing our repairs at Cape Town *Statesman* proceeded towards Durban to take up salvage station. On arrival we moored at our usual berth. Painting and general maintenance work was carried out by our crew.

Some crew members were invited ashore to barbecues but only on condition they left a telephone number. Myself and Keith Appleyard, our wireless operator, we were confined to stay aboard. After all we were on salvage station.

One evening Keith came to my cabin saying there was a ship on fire in the Mozambique channel. So with our crew rounded up we set sail. I never knew the ship's name (*Antonia Xilas)* but he was in trouble alright. Their cargo of coal was alight and on our arrival we found that the whole ship was ablaze and trailing behind the vessel on a long wire was their crew sat inside a lifeboat.

Antonia Xilas
Photo copyright Fred Fletcher.

I asked the Greek master if he would like our assistance in putting out the fire, also would you and your crew care to come aboard? He refused point blank and said a Dutch tug was only a few hours away and they had been contracted to assist. All I could do was standby. Three hours later a Dutch tug arrived, *Witte Zee*, and making connection to the burning vessel commenced towing towards Madagascar, intending to beach the vessel.

Witte Zee
Photo copyright Fred Fletcher.

We wasn't going anywhere so I hung around to watch the operation. When the smoking Greek was beached it started leaking bunker oil onto the lovely snow white beach apparently used by tourists. A police launch approached the Dutch tug and arrested them for beaching the smouldering hulk without permission. So we sneaked away back to Durban post haste.

Antonia Xilas
Photo copyright Fred Fletcher.

So back in Durban to our berth and we continued our daily routine etc. We got to know quite a lot of the locals. When United Towing bought the *Statesman* from the Moran Towing Co. of New York she was registered under the Liberian flag, so for reasons unknown United never put her under the red ensign. However, one day the Durban Harbour Master came aboard *Statesman* asking why I wasn't flying a national flag. I replied that I'm not keen on flying the Liberian flag on a British ship.

The only clean and good looking flag we had was New Zealand so we both agreed whilst moored inside Durban we could fly the New Zealand flag. It looked better flying above a freshly painted *Statesman*.

Anita Monti

We spent four weeks moored at Durban when, just after supper one night, Keith the wireless operator picked up a distress call from a super tanker called *Anita Monti* saying she was on fire in her engine room. We immediately set sail and at the same time informed United Towing of the situation. They came back saying that *Statesman* had got the contract.

Turned out that *Anita Monti* was inside the Mozambique channel and drifting. Next morning we arrived and the *Anita Monti's* Captain had lowered a six inch mooring rope over his bow and asked me to take hold of it for towing. I explained to him that it was too small, however he insisted so I had to prove it to him, and yes it parted. He then said that they had no power for heaving our heavy towing gear aboard. I explained to him that it wasn't a problem. So passing a messenger aboard *Anita Monti's* bow, around his mooring bollards and back to the tug, that way the tug could heave the tow aboard, which is what we did.

Our towing gear consisted of 75 fathoms of 20cm wire. shackled to that was a nylon towing spring of braid line material straight onto *Statesman's* towing winch. All connected and we commenced towing. *Anita Monti's* steering gear was stuck at ten degrees to port causing an awkward sheer and making towing difficult. However the sea was flat calm so it wasn't too bad but it was going to be a problem if the weather turned nasty.

We had only been towing for six hours, making six knots, when we parted from *Anita Monti*. I was very puzzled as to why, so quickly we hove our towing gear aboard, only to discover that the nylon spring's splice had pulled out. The braid line splicing system was entirely different to standard splicing, I explained to *Anita Monti's* Captain and said I'll soon be back alongside.

I was annoyed at the splice pulling out and instructed the mate to dump the remains of the spring overboard whilst our engines were stopped. After rigging fresh towing gear we decided to return to *Anita Monti's* position to reconnect.

Anita Monti
Photo taken from *Statesman*, copyright Eddie Barker.

I had just put our engines to slow ahead when a loud banging sound came from below. I was told by my engineers that our propellers were fouled. Head in hand I thought what the hell had caused the fouling? Some of our lads, swimming trunks on, dived over the stern and told me that the old spring had caught onto the rudder post.

By this time German and Dutch tugs had arrived on the scene and when I tried to make conversation with *Anita Monti's* Captain to explain just what had happened they started jamming our conversation.

Whilst we attempted to clear our propellers the Captain of *Anita Monti* came aboard via a small powered dinghy. This Italian Captain viewed our situation up and seeing his tanker was now in no danger decided to wait for us. He was very annoyed at the German and Dutch tugs, or one of them, for jamming our messages and he told them so.

Now clearing the propeller was a work of art to say the least. Our diver wasn't available so running a pipe down to the engine room compressor and into a face mask Judd, our greaser (whom I had dumped gash over his head earlier) volunteered to make the first dive.

So with hacksaw blades plus galley knife we took it in turns to dive and hack away the fouled propeller. Our company had chartered a helicopter with divers to come but after twelve hours the propellers were clear - mostly due to Judd.

Some of *Statesman's* crew members.
L to R. Dave Boulton AB, Stan (Robinson?) greaser, Mick Jurkiewicz AB,
Pete Maltby (Judd) greaser, Robin Dvelis deck cadet.
Photo UTSS collection.

The helicopter cancelled we reconnected to *Anita Monti* and this time minus a nylon spring we set off again. Our destination was to be Simon's Town, just south of Cape Town which was roughly twelve hundred miles away.

We encountered heavy weather and with *Anita Monti's* jammed rudder, it was arranged that when passing Durban a helicopter would be flying out some spares for *Anita Monti* and fitters to try and get the steering gear fixed.

Sure enough steering sorted out made a hell of a difference to our speed. It meant that now *Anita Monti* could steer behind the tug.

We encountered some heavy weather and strong currents but finally arrived in False Bay off Simon's Town, an ex naval base, and anchored after *Anita Monti* had been safely anchored.

After we bunkered and stored up we had to standby *Anita Monti* until a decision was made as to whether she could repair at Cape Town. Then came the news that *Anita Monti*, after token repairs, was to be towed to Marseilles in France, a six thousand mile tow.

We heard that *Englishman* was on passage to our location to assist in the towing to Marseilles. Also United Towing was nearing completion of a new tug called *Lloydsman*, which if completed in time was to meet us on passage.

Dirch Maersk

Another twist to this story - whilst standing by *Anita Monti* a Danish super tanker was making slow speed towards Cape Town and asked if we was available to assist. *Anita Monti's* Captain agreed but only when *Englishman* arrived. She was due in a few hours time.

So when *Englishman* arrived off we went to the *Dirch Maersk*. On arrival they asked if we would make fast as a precaution.

Dirch Maersk
Photo taken from *Statesman*, copyright Eddie Barker.

We arrived at Cape Town after only a seventy mile tow, topped our bunkers up and went back to Simon's Town in time for the long tow to Marseilles after re-connecting to *Anita Monti*. We then commenced towing along with the *Englishman*.

Statesman leaving False Bay towing *Anita Monti*
Photo taken from *Englishman*, copyright Ernie Parker.

At the beginning we were making a good speed then off Walvis Bay we encountered strong head winds and currents which reduced our speed quite a lot. We were only making five to six knots but we plodded onwards. After ten days news came saying that *Lloydsman* had finished building at Leith in Scotland and was steaming towards us to relieve *Englishman*.

The day came when *Lloydsman* finally arrived, commanded by Capt. Arthur King, an old friend of mine. After she had connected and *Englishman* departed for Cape Town away we went.

Lloydsman, having just taken over the tow from *Englishman*
Photo taken from *Englishman*, copyright Ernie Parker.

Lloydsman's extra power made all the difference. The combined power of *Statesman* and *Lloydsman* gave us a speed of eight knots. The captain of *Anita Monti* said to both tugs "If you arrive at Marseilles for Christmas there's a case of wine each." We answered "It's a deal." After the long drag we arrived at Marseilles two days before Christmas and, true to his word, we got our cases of wine. Everybody was very pleased that we had arrived okay.

Next day *Anita Monti* was to be berthed at the oil terminal but now we heard that the local tugs were on strike - what now? After discussing the situation further King and myself suggested to *Anita Monti* that we would try and berth her ourselves.

Now we had *Statesman* made fast forward and *Lloydsman's* bow made fast to *Anita Monti's* stern. Whilst approaching a narrow channel I asked *Lloydsman* to take some way off. So *Lloydsman* went astern with his engines but, low and behold, his fore bollard flew off. This panicked the French pilot and he refused to go any further – not that I blamed him. So I managed to turn *Anita Monti* around and go back to anchor.

Over the Christmas period we made merry aboard *Anita Monti*. We now realised the local tug strike was to last quite a long time, so the powers that be decided we were to proceed to tow *Anita Monti* to Palermo in Sicily. By this time Arthur King, Captain of the *Lloydsman* was relieved by Capt. Norman Story for the short tow to Palermo, Sicily.

The day came when we set off towards Palermo. The day before we arrived there I was told that myself and the crew were to be relieved on arrival at Palermo. Our crew had been aboard *Statesman* for seven months. After saying goodbye to the Captain of *Anita Monti* we made our way back to the U.K. via Rome.

Funny thing at Rome, Judd our famous greaser got himself well and truly drunk and laid out on a bench at Rome airport. Our flight was due out in thirty minutes and I knew they wouldn't allow him aboard the plane in that state so, sticking his plane ticket inside his pocket I left him there. I never had a choice, I had the rest of the crew to consider.

Lloydsman & *Statesman* towing *Anita Monti*
Photo taken from *Englishman*, copyright Ernie Parker.

Nevertheless Judd turned up back home a few days later large as life. Deep down you couldn't help liking Judd because away from drink he was a very hard working lad and this I told our boss on arrival back home. He was given a large bonus also for his help in clearing *Statesman's* propellers.

Chief Officer Fred Fletcher ready to connect to *Anita Monti*
Photo copyright Eddie Barker

Chapter 8
1972 – 1976 - *Statesman (1969)*, *Euroman (1972)* and the Cod Wars

I did various jobs, mainly moving oil rigs around the North Sea. Then, at the beginning of 1972, the second cod war broke out between our government and the Icelandic government. This involved myself as now I was back in command of *Statesman*. After moving an oil rig one day I was expecting to return to Hull when orders came from United's office to proceed to Leith in Scotland.

On arriving at Leith we were then told that we were going up to Iceland to act as a "buffer tug". This meant that if gun boats of the Icelandic coast guard try to cut a trawlers warps then my job was to come between the gun boat and the trawler, at least that was the idea. Because *Statesman* was a solid piece of metal compared to gun boats which really were paper thin in comparison we had few skirmishes. *Statesman* was on her own apart from *Miranda*. She was engaged as a hospital ship.

January 1973, *Statesman's* crew in Leith just before leaving for Iceland
The first tug to be involved in the Cod Wars
Photo copyright The Daily Telegraph.

I used to cruise up and down doing our best to stave off the gun boats, a few near misses but nothing really serious.

UK Government representative (Support Commander) Ted Turner.
Capt. Turner was himself a former Master of *Statesman*
Photo UTSS collection.

We used to trade meat and bacon for fresh caught fish from some of the trawlers but some of the conditions those fishermen worked in was appalling to say the least. Icing up, rigging all iced up, some used to fish regardless of the state of the weather, gutting fish and throwing them down open hatches. I was expecting at times to see a wave go down these hatches but nothing ever happened. They were used to it I suppose. After a few trips in *Statesman* the cod war ceased temporarily but erupted again later in 1975.

Euroman (1972)

After a four week leave I was engaged in oil rig work in the North Sea, such as moving oil rigs from location to location. Since I had been in South Africa United had purchased a tug from the Germans. Its former name being *Bremen*, United renamed her *Euroman*.

One day I was asked to join *Euroman* and do some rig moving. She was single screw with a Kort nozzle, this being her propeller inside a casing so as to give more power. She was seven thousand horse power.

Euroman (1972) [Bremen (1967)]
Photo UTSS collection.

Now an oil rig was being built at Greenock in Scotland called *Alitihad* and *Lloydsman* was to tow her to the Persian Gulf. But *Lloydsman* was refitting at Lisbon so we in *Euroman* were told to make for Greenock and commence towing this oil rig down the Irish Sea towards Lands End where *Lloydsman* was supposed to meet us and take over the tow.

On we sailed through the Bay of Biscay, still no sign of *Lloydsman*. However she eventually caught us up at Dakar, North West Africa. The Captain of *Lloydsman* was Captain Cyril Hyam, another good friend of mine, and after handing over the oil rig I expected to return to Hull. But fresh orders were received, we were to proceed to the Bonnie River, West Africa, to tow an oil rig across the Atlantic to Port Arthur, Texas, U.S.A.

On seeing this rig, *Sedco Four,* I thought, hell I've never seen a rig as small as this one. Should be an easy tow, no problem. Things turned out quite different though as I will try to explain. This oil rig was specially built to drill in shallow waters and on soft bottoms such as soft mud, this we didn't know at the time of sailing, but once we got under way we soon found out.

After sailing we could only make three knots towing full speed. After further inquiries it was found that the oil rig was welded onto a very large barge so that when drilling onto soft mud the rig would not sink too far into the soft bottom. This made a hell of a difference to our speed, also this large barge hadn't been out of the water for a number of years, it must have been covered all over in growth - mud and barnacles. I informed United Towing of the situation and was told to carry on regardless.

After towing for a few days things got a little better because maybe some of the mud had washed away. But towing a large barge under water was bound to be a drag. We was slightly north of the equator, I was hoping to pick up the currents that are supposed to flow from east to west.

We struggled along for over four thousand miles, our first destination was to be Trinidad but I was worried about our bunker situation. Worst of all we started to run short of drinking water so I had to start rationing the water, to some moans and groans. About a hundred miles from Trinidad the drinking water was becoming desperate. We took the lids off the water tanks and bucketed it out that way.

I had only enough fuel to last as well. I informed United Towing office about our predicament, they told me that Arthur Whitley, our new Engineering Superintendent was flying out to Trinidad to arrange something for us on arrival.

In the end our water situation was desperate. Some of the crew started draining the radiators and making coffee with the water. We got to about fifty miles from Trinidad when a small tug was spotted on the horizon coming towards us. I was just about to ask them for some fresh water when Arthur Whitley's voice blurted out over the radio saying he was aboard of the little tug and that he had brought us some cases of bottled water. We've never appreciated water as much as we did that day!

We managed it to the anchorage in Trinidad. We had winch trouble so were stuck there for a few days. Incidentally it turned out that *Euroman* had only twelve hours of fuel left on board on arrival at Trinidad.

After repairs were completed we set off to complete the rest of our journey to Port Arthur in Texas where my relief, Capt. Jack Linford took over command. We all flew home for a well earned rest.

Euroman sailed straight home to Hull for a full refit. After our leave I was engaged in various jobs. I did a little tow in my old tug the *Masterman,* a bucket dredger from Falmouth to Liverpool, and other coastal work.

Third Cod War, November 1975.

We were hearing on the radio and television that arguments between Iceland and Britain had broken out again. The British fishermen were demanding protection from the Royal Navy. I was personally wondering whether buffer tugs would be needed again. I was soon to find out.

Euroman was ready for sea again and guess what? I joined her again and yes, buffer tugs were needed again.

Our first orders were to proceed up North to the Port of Rosyth in Scotland, a naval base then. I was taken ashore and was told all about our role regarding buffer tugs. I already knew from last time but I had to sign the Official Secrets Act. I was given secret details regarding Icelandic gun boats and personal likes and dislikes of the gun boat skippers. For instance one particular Captain had a girlfriend in a port called Seydisfjord, so we may find his gun boat in that area. Charming I thought, I wondered if they had my past history as well.

So away we went back up to Iceland on 29th November 1975. This was one date I can remember as it was a friend of mines birthday in Rosyth. So after 800 miles of lousy weather we arrived back off Iceland.

We had on board a special chart marked out in fishing zones like an A to Z marked in squares. Also a frigate was on station in one of these zones. I was told to go and patrol in one of these zones and to keep the frigate informed of any movements and, most of all, restrict them from passing information to the media. At first I was on station off Langaness on one corner of Iceland and had to report any trawlers that strayed inside special limits agreed such as say 12 miles, I'm not quite sure. Plus protecting trawlers from having their warps cut by Icelandic gun boats.

I'd only been on station for about four days guarding a bunch of trawlers when an Icelandic gun boat appeared and demanded that the trawlers stop fishing. The gun boats name was *Thor* so I kept pretty close to the *Thor* to try to anticipate his next move. Then I noticed him streaming out his wire cutting gear. I kept him in sight all the time steaming pretty close together then *Thor* came hard to port across *Euroman's* bow thinking I would be tempted to go full astern. I'm afraid I just kept going and my bow collided with *Thor's* port quarter where his cutting winch was situated thus damaging the winch. His wire started running out and he lost all of his winch wire overboard. I reported by secret code to the Royal Navy frigate, they asked if *Euroman* was okay, I replied "Yes."

Now when *Euroman* was built she had an ice breaking bow for breaking ice in the Baltic, so no way was I worried about damaging myself. The *Thor*, after a few choice words, returned to port, most likely for repairs to his winch.

The Icelandic government had quite a few gun boats on hand. Some trawlers further south had their fishing gear out so this meant that another buffer tug was sent.

My old tug *Statesman*. Included was another frigate but the navy was restricted to how far they could go. Their hulls were very thin, their only advantage was speed and guns which they could not use unless a trawler was fired upon, then things would have been different.

When things were a bit quiet up North I used to break ice for trawlers to continue fishing but, sure enough, a few days later we were visited by another gun boat called *Aegir*. This gun boat was very fast indeed, he cut two trawlers warps and away he went, I just never had his speed. After a month we sailed to Greenock in Scotland for a relief crew to take over and for us to take some leave.

Icelandic Coastguard Cutter *Odinn*
Photo copyright Fred Fletcher.

Next time we joined *Euroman* again it was at the Shetland Islands. We flew from Leeds airport direct to Lerwick, and so back on board *Euroman* and up to Iceland again. This time we embarked a naval ex-Commander to represent the government on arrival at the Whale Back which is a rock sticking out of the sea six miles off the coast of Iceland. The reason it's called Whale Back is because it resembles a whale, especially when seas pound it.

By now ships such as the navy, plus *Englishman, Welshman* and *Euroman*, even a Nimrod plane flew over regularly as a spotter plane, but I preferred to be on my own away from the armada. Then came my next encounter with an Icelandic gun boat. My old friend the *Aegir*.

I now had a system where I would lay amongst the trawlers with no deck lights showing, sometimes switching navigation lights off temporarily. This particular night the *Aegir* came dashing in with his cutter streamed out, only this time I came into contact with the *Aegir* with my port shoulder. Such was the bump that the gun boat laid right over to starboard. I could even see her propeller and rolling chock as she keeled over. However she soon righted herself. They then pointed their gun at us but that's all they did do - just as well. Some newspaper reporters came to Iceland to report whatever they could but I would never allow them aboard *Euroman*.

One particular day *Lloydsman* appeared in a blaze of glory loaded down with T.V. reporters from the B.B.C., plus newspaper reporters. Norman Story was Master of *Lloydsman* at this time. She had just returned from a long distance tow and on arrival at Hull he had joined her. He asked me if I would like a reporter to come aboard but I promptly replied "No thank you, you can have them all with pleasure."

So off I went to the north again in company with *Statesman*. Some trawlers were complaining that tugs patrolling at night time resembled Icelandic gun boats so some bright spark suggested fitting blue flashing lights on the tugs masthead. All very nice but now the gun boats knew exactly where the tugs were as they looked like police cars flashing away. *Euroman* was fitted with such a light but I never used it.

The Icelandic coast guard knew exactly where *Lloydsman* was because her radio was blurting out all the time, especially the newspaper reporters reporting back home to their editors. *Lloydsman* was named the news desk after that. I believe the Icelandic coast guard was keeping a strict surveillance on *Lloydsman* because of her publishing. One day a couple of supply boats arrived to join the armada. Now most seafarers know that supply boats carry a lot of water aboard for transferring to oil rigs. So when it was found that *Lloydsman* was in need of some fresh water, what with all her now extra crew using it, she requested some to be transferred to her. But the weather as it was at the time made it impossible where they where.

Now we all was told to keep clear of the 12 mile limit but between themselves *Lloydsman* and the supply boat ignored this order, and under cover of darkness, went inshore to transfer the water under the lee of the land. Silently watching all this was the Icelandic coast guard.

An Icelandic gun boat crept along the coast with marines on board, they then made a dash towards *Lloydsman* but the supply boat had spotted the gun boat coming and took off quick. *Lloydsman* was very lucky this time. The gun boat tried to board *Lloydsman* and arrest her but the swell prevented this so they both bumped alongside each other and fell away. *Lloydsman* managed to escape but the navy and Prime Minister Callaghan were furious. It was touch and go whether *Lloydsman* returned to the U.K. but the incident soon blew over. Years after this story has changed quite a bit as some people know, but they wasn't there!

In 1976 the powers that be, being Iceland and the U.K. came to some sort of agreement that ended the so called Cod War. Some say that the Americans had something to do with it, Iceland being a member of NATO. However I'd had enough of Iceland so I was pleased about it really.

After returning to the U.K. we were informed that *Euroman* was for sale. She was, to me, a comfortable boat to be on but for North Sea work she wasn't suitable. She was single screw and with no fancy bow thrust so, after leave, I was elected to show foreign buyers around *Euroman* and to tell them how good she was.

She was finally bought by a Greek firm and sailed to Greece. I think Captain Jack Linford sailed with the tug to show the Greeks how to run her, followed by a Skipper called Ken Bishoprick. As for myself I was back aboard *Statesman*, moving and standing by oil rigs in the North Sea.

1977 - Captain Charles Noble MBE.

It was while towing an oil rig out from Stavanger that the new year honours list was broadcast and low and behold my name was amongst the list. At the time I was hove to in a severe gale so I wasn't that impressed.

We returned to Hull and I went to our office. Everybody was congratulating me, I'd been awarded an M.B.E. but I wasn't that impressed. I told our office that I'm not keen on the idea but was told that it would be good for the company as well if I accepted it. So come 7th March 1977 I made my way to a London hotel. The next day was going to be the day of the investiture at Buckingham Palace.

CENTRAL CHANCERY OF THE ORDERS OF KNIGHTHOOD
ST JAMES'S PALACE, SW1A 1BG
TELEPHONE - 01-834 2837 & 2838

INVESTITURE "E"   28th January 1977

Sir,

I am commanded to inform you that an Investiture will be held at Buckingham Palace on Tuesday, 8th March, 1977, at which your attendance is requested.

I am desired to say that you should arrive at the Palace between the hours of 10 o'clock and 10.30 a.m. and this letter should be shown on entering the gates of the Palace, as no other card of admission is issued to recipients. Cars may be parked in the inner Quadrangle of the Palace under police direction. No windscreen tickets are issued.

If desired, two guests are permitted to accompany you to watch the Ceremony, and tickets for them may be obtained by making application on the form enclosed herewith which should be returned to me as soon as possible.

The only exception to this rule is that, if a recipient wishes to bring with him his wife and two sons, or two daughters, or a son and daughter, a third ticket will be issued, but in NO circumstances will a fourth ticket be issued.

DRESS

(a) Serving Officers and Other Ranks of the Royal Navy, Army, Royal Air Force and Members of the Police Force and Fire Brigades should wear the dress laid down in the regulations of their respective Service. Decorations and Medals should not be worn; nor should swords be worn.

(b) Retired Officers who are not in possession of the dress described in (a) should wear Morning Dress or Dark Lounge Suit. Orders, Decorations and Medals should not be worn.

(c) Civilians may, *if they so desire*, wear the uniform of the Civil Organization or Service to which they belong; otherwise they should wear Morning Dress or Dark Lounge Suit. Orders, Decorations and Medals should not be worn.

I am, Sir,

Your obedient servant,

Secretary.

Charles H. Noble, Esq., MBE

Now before leaving home I'd sent my uniform jacket to the cleaners, not my trousers because they didn't need it. However when the uniform jacket returned back from the cleaners wrapped up in a plastic type bag I put it straight into my suitcase but forgot to add the trousers. The night before the ceremony we decided to have a dress rehearsal, it was then that we discovered no trousers - what now? I was all for returning home but the wife, Valerie, insisted on trying to obtain some. First she asked the porter but to no avail, you couldn't blame him, some woman asking for trousers! Then the police, no good there either. The hotel did say that up the street was a tailor but he didn't open until nine o'clock the next morning. Only thing was that we had to be at the palace for ten o'clock.

We were waiting outside the tailors shop for him to open. When he came to the shop we explained our predicament. He more or less found a perfect match to the uniform jacket. So we went back to the hotel, got dressed to kill and made the palace with ten minutes to spare.

Charlie outside the palace with his wife Val and Mother-in-Law.
Resplendent in his new trousers and medal.
Photo Hull Daily Mail.

Statesman (1969)

My next assignment was to fly out to Egypt to relieve the *Statesman's* crew. We flew out to Cairo then went by a dirty truck to Suez, then aboard the *Statesman* to relieve the crew. We almost had to sail immediately for the Saudi Arabian port of Jeddah. Our tow was a cargo ferry, I can't remember the name [Seaspeed Dora] but she was only nine months old. She had arrived from the U.K. with lorries, cars and Land Rovers all stacked above decks.

Seaspeed Dora, before salvage.
Photo UTSS collection.

Whilst discharging her cargo of cars etc. they started taking on bunkers through a doorway on the ships side which was just above the water line. Instead of discharging the top deck section first the local dock workers started discharging the bottom half first causing the vessel to list sharply to port, thereby putting the bunker hatch under water. It wasn't long before the vessel flooded and keeled over sinking, but she was in shallow water so only half of the vessel was showing above water.

Seaspeed Dora, under tow.
Photo UTSS collection.

Her cargo of new cars and lorries was a mangled heap. Apparently a Greek salvage company had salvaged the vessel and got her upright.

The Greeks had a tug working with them, turned out to be the old *Euroman* which United Towing had sold to them some weeks before. [Now named *Petrola's Ocean Master 24*]

Petrola's Ocean Master 24 [Euroman (1972)] [Bremen (1967)]
Photo copyright unknown - Public domain.

We sailed up the Red Sea and on to Suez. The Egyptian authorities would not allow us to tow the vessel through the Suez Canal until they had inspected the vessel which took days to complete. Then after the inspection they wanted cash payment up front to pay for canal fees and tug assistance, so that took a week to complete. Came the day we joined a convoy of ships going through the canal but had to wait until the last vessel had entered, then it was our turn to join.

We arrived at the halfway mark, being the Bitter Lakes, but we had to anchor with our tow because the local tug that had been assisting us disappeared during the night. Now we had to wait until the next day until another tug could be found. We eventually made it through to Port Said and away to Greece, the Port of Athens, where we handed our tow to local tugs. I was pleased to see the back of it. Our crew were due for relief so a new crew arrived, but no skipper for my relief.

We was told to sail as soon as possible to assist one of our own tugs, *Welshman* that had broken adrift from her tow near Sardinia.

They were bound for Barcelona and somehow were unable to reconnect. So with a new crew we set off for their location. It took us five days to reach the *Welshman* and on arrival we managed to connect and tow the vessel stern first to Barcelona with *Welshman* escorting.

It was in Barcelona that I was relieved and flew home for some leave.

Chapter 9
December 1977 - *Lloydsman (1971)*

Venpet

Whilst on leave I heard on the television that two large super tankers had collided off South Africa. One was called *Venpet* and the other *Venoil*. Both were sister ships with a tonnage of 153,000 tons each. Apparently *Venpet* caught fire. *Lloydsman* was on station at the time of the collision and went to their assistance. *Venoil* did not require assistance so *Venpet*, after the fire was extinguished was escorted into Cape Town by the *Lloydsman.*

Captain Linford was Master of *Lloydsman* on this occasion and what's more Jack Linford was due for relief, and guess who had to relieve him?

I got my orders to relieve Capt. Linford so after flying out to Cape Town I joined the *Lloydsman*. After settling down in the *Lloydsman* I went to have a look at the *Venpet*. She was huge and so was the hole in her starboard quarter, all blackened with the fire. I thought she would take some repairing but all they did was make her seaworthy, cementing the inner bulkhead, but the outer skin was left.

She was too large for the local dry dock to further more repairs. The cause of the collision I was told was that *Venoil* was trying to come alongside of the *Venpet*, for what reason nobody could find out.

Rumours were spreading that a German tug was going to be chartered to tow the *Venpet* to Singapore or maybe Japan. I thought at the time that *Venpet* would take some towing especially with that hole not too far above the water line. After lying at Cape Town for a month our office had a tow for us, and sure enough that tow was to be *Venpet*.

A runner crew was sent out from the UK. to crew the *Venpet*. I asked our office if a Superintendent was coming out to view their new contract and was politely told no, we will leave it in your good hands. I was quite surprised because as usual someone used to inspect most tows before accepting the contract. After storing and rigging the *Venpet* for sea we finally set off.

Local tugs brought *Venpet* out of the harbour and in the main stream outside the harbour we connected and our long tow commenced.

Our final destination was Nagasaki in Japan. At first we had to struggle with the wind and currents that are constant around the South African coast, but eventually clear of the currents we headed out into the Indian Ocean. Our speed increased slightly, we could only make 4 knots. Each day we had to report our progress to our office.

First they complained at the speed we was making so we increased our speed to 4 -1/2 knots but that also made an increase in our fuel consumption. A couple of days later after giving our daily report to head office they came back to say that our fuel consumption was too high! I mentioned that we can't have it both ways. One or the other.

We plodded on regardless then we found out that our water making machine had broken down. All we could do was some sort of rationing, being that we turned the water pumps off twice a day, putting them on for one hour in the morning and also for one hour at night. Some of the crew moaned and groaned but it had to be done for everyone's sake. We got showered in the tropical rain that fell regularly.

Day after day dragged on. The largest cause of our slow speed was during a heavy swell. Although the sea was calm enough the swell seemed to come from nowhere. When the *Venpet's* stern dipped into the swell the sea rushed into the large damaged hole and caused a drag through the hole which in turn reduced our speed to 2 knots. When the swell died down it was back to 4 knots. But more was to come.

Lloydsman towing *Venpet*, the huge damage clearly seen.
Photo copyright unknown – Public domain.

We ran into a severe gale from the west. Now there is nothing worse than a gale or any wind coming from the beam whilst towing a tanker, mainly because the *Venpet* was riding high out of the water but the main trouble is her large funnel and bridge. Once the wind catches these objects, especially when they are at the stern of the vessel they act as a rudder and a sail thus causing *Venpet* to head into the wind all the time.

This gale went on for very nearly a week. We were going nowhere fast and at one time *Venpet* was towing *Lloydsman* astern. All we could do was pay out more winch wire and just lay ahead of *Venpet* which just dragged us stern first. I was just pleased that we were a thousand miles from any land or things would have been serious indeed.

We had blown astern for a hundred miles then the wind ceased quite suddenly so we commenced plodding on. The drinking water was lasting quite well so I was pleased about that. I used to sit out on deck most evenings just worrying about what could go wrong next.

Our wireless operator, called Sanderson, used to sit with us swapping yarns. He turned out to be a good friend to me in more ways than one. He was the spitting image of a brother of mine.

So back to our speed which averaged between four to sometimes five knots. It was arranged for us to take on fuel oil at Djakarta, Indonesia but I couldn't help worrying about passing through the Sunda Straights narrow passage.

Came the day we sailed through okay without any problems. An Indonesian supply boat was to take over *Venpet* whilst *Lloydsman* took on bunkers and stores. So passing over my towing gear to the supply boat we entered Djakarta harbour, but United Towing told me to inform the *Lloydsman's* crew that it wasn't at all possible to relieve them there and that the local government would not allow this to happen. This turned out to be a lie because just lying ahead of us on the quay was a British ship also changing crew, and some of our crew found out.

Next I knew was that I was summoned to the British Embassy in Djakarta and politely told that I had to relieve our crew because the ships articles stated that after six months crews will be relieved. So informing our office in Hull they then agreed to fly a fresh crew out to us but would our crew agree to sail just outside the harbour to reconnect to the *Venpet* and discharge the supply vessel. This meant me dodging up and down in the Java Sea slowly holding *Venpet* to tide. This went on for six long days hoping that the weather wouldn't turn nasty.

A launch came alongside and crews changed over to my relief so once again we started our second voyage to Japan and now plenty of fresh water to take a shower when I wanted.

So now was the final trek to Japan which turned out to be a smooth passage. Our speed increased to five knots. Whether the current was with us or more so a new engineer I don't really know. By now my health was beginning to affect me, my breathing was getting worse.

Still we plodded on, then came the day we arrived at Nagasaki. It was great when our tow wire was cast off and *Venpet* was anchored - journeys end.

Our towing distance from Cape Town to Nagasaki was a total 8,749 miles, a total of 88 days towing, also our fuel consumption was 1691 tons. I was so glad to step off the *Lloydsman* for the very last time. I hated every bit of that trip.

So we booked into a hotel for the night after handing over command of the Lloydsman to Captain John Garrod. Next day we were put aboard a flight back home via Alaska.

My breathing was getting worse, I know I should have seen a doctor in Japan but all I wanted was to get home as quickly as possible. I think the stress of this voyage was taking its toll. At one time on the aircraft I was so bad I tried to open my button on my shirt but couldn't do it. There was no oxygen aboard the aircraft, the stewards asked everyone to stop smoking.

The aircraft arrived at Hamburg in Germany. An ambulance was waiting to take me to hospital on arrival. I was given oxygen to help me breathe. I'd had a bad asthma attack. I was injected with something that made me feel a lot better. They wanted to keep me in the German hospital but I just wanted to get home. So leaving the hospital I flew to Heathrow, London and the wife was waiting to ferry me home by car along with our wireless operator Sandy as we called him. Sandy never left my side during my illness.

We arrived back at Hull dropping Sandy off first. I met his mother who informed me that her maiden name was Noble. I thought when I first met Sandy that he resembled a brother of mine so maybe way back we might have been related?

Chapter 10
1978 - *Seaman (1967), Englishman (1965)*

Seaman (1967)

It wasn't long before I was taken ill again only this time I spent eight weeks in hospital with bronchial asthma. On coming out of hospital it wasn't long before I was back aboard a tug again, only this was a much smaller tug called *Seaman*, same name as my very first tug. We was to work at Kishorn, Scotland. They were building a very large oil platform, Ninian Central [7] made out of concrete that resembled a concrete cooling tower which you see near power stations. I enjoyed working at Loch Kishorn because it was day work which suited me fine. We were transporting concrete in special barges to the rig.

It was interesting to see it slowly grow day by day. Then came the day the concrete rig was finished and was towed away, and we returned to Hull.

Ninian Central Platform under construction at Loch Kishorn.
Photo copyright Ernie Parker.

Ninian Central Platform under tow to North Sea location.
Photo copyright unknown – Public domain.

[7] From Kishorn Port Ltd. Website.

As the Ninian project continued it was floated out into Loch Kishorn, at that time it weighed close to 150,000 tonnes. The wet dock in Loch Kishorn has an almost unlimited depth for construction purposes at 80 metres. Upon completion the 600,000 tonne concrete platform was towed by seven tugs to its North Sea location. At that time this was the largest man-made moveable object.

Englishman (1965)

It wasn't long before I was off again, this time to Trinidad to take command of *Englishman*. I also heard *Statesman* was sold whilst I was working at Kishorn and *Lloydsman* was soon to follow.

At Trinidad I was only aboard two days before we went to the assistance of a German coastal vessel which we towed in to Trinidad. We then spent several weeks doing nothing much until a Greek ship loaded with sugar had lost his propeller and wanted towing to Caracas, Venezuela. So away we went and towed this Greek vessel to Caracas. On arrival I went aboard to get signed up and found she was alive with rats. I never lingered very long, straight back aboard the *Englishman* I went.

We sailed back to Trinidad and the German ship we had towed in early in our trip had to be towed back to Florida where she was built. We towed the German vessel as far as Cuba, that's when we experienced a typhoon. Seas like mountains but we somehow managed to keep hold of our tow.

The storm blew itself out and we eventually arrived at Florida, 'Land of the Free' - I don't think so. Our crew wasn't allowed ashore, the excuse was that we never had any visas to land on American soil. They even put an armed guard at the bottom of the gangway. They said I could visit our agent ashore. I told them our agent could visit me aboard. Anyhow back to Trinidad we sailed.

During the trip back to Trinidad *Englishman* developed engine problems which meant sailing on one engine, being twin screw, it wasn't a problem. So while our engineers were repairing the engine our chief engineer Ernie Parker disconnected the damaged engine propeller shaft so the propeller could freely turn whilst running through the passage back to Trinidad. It wasn't to be as simple as that.

The gearbox for the free disconnected propeller was somehow badly damaged and on arrival at Trinidad our chief and myself were relieved and flew home to explain what had happened. Our chief was made redundant, I really felt sorry for him. It seemed a new brush was sweeping United's office staff. Ex supply boat skippers were starting to become experts in towing or so they thought. All they had ever done was skipper supply boats. Their sole purpose was supplying oil rigs with fuel and water, they were twin screw vessels, plus bow thrust - anybody's granny could work those boats.

Captain Hopper had retired. He was an ex master in ocean towing. When at sea, any problems we had we could always rely on Captain Hopper to give us good advice but these new comedians now in United Towing's office never had a clue. They were fresh master mariners from school looking for a soft job. I now know why that when I towed the *Venpet* from South Africa to Japan nobody came from United's office to advise or represent our company's interests.

Chapter 11
1982 - The Falklands War, *Irishman (1978)*

I could see the writing on the wall for a once proud towing company. Some new tugs were built for the oil industry, twin screw, bow thrusters, these were very comfortable tugs to work especially when you had been used to just single screw.

They replaced the old single screw tugs gradually but still they could not get experienced tug masters. Some came from Liverpool, most had a lot of experience but some ex supply boat skippers hadn't a clue and now with the office staff having very little knowledge United Towing was losing contracts from a lot of sources. This was mainly because of cock-ups made by these inexperienced new breed of tug masters who, if their bow thrusts wouldn't work, were up the creek without a paddle. It was sad for me to see this happening. I used to be proud to be a tug master but the direction the company was now going in was anybody's guess.

In 1982 United was saved for the time being. As everybody knows Argentina invaded the Falkland Islands and a task force sailed south. I was Captain of the tug *Irishman*, working in the North Sea, and we were due for relief. We got orders to sail to Portsmouth where a relief crew was waiting to join. It was then that we went on leave, the new crew joined and Irishman headed south to the Ascension Islands to wait until the task force was ready, when they eventually sailed towards the Falkland Islands.

Whilst the Falklands war was being fought the tugs were kept at sea on standby. The *Atlantic Conveyor* had been hit by an Exocet missile and was a wreck and a danger to shipping so *Irishman* was ordered to tow her well away from the danger zone. Two of *Irishman's* deck crew boarded the *Atlantic Conveyor* to make a tow but sadly the *Atlantic Conveyor* sank. The two deck crew were awarded British Empire Medals medal for going aboard and making the tug fast.

Dennis Betts & Garry Bales.
Awarded the B.E.M. for the attempted salvage of the *Atlantic Conveyor.*
Photo Garry Bales collection.

It was then after the conflict that tugs were allowed into Port Stanley and it was then that I flew out via Hercules transport plane to rejoin the *Irishman*.

Irishman (1978)
Photo UTSS collection.

Relief crew for *Irishman*, Charlie seen bottom right.
Photo copyright Hull Daily Mail.

Our first job was to tow the *St. Tristan* landing craft from San Carlos Bay to Port Stanley, then the real work started in earnest. Ships were arriving regularly loaded with building materials to build a road to a new airport that was being built. It was non stop but for most of the time it was daylight hours. Except when we were on manoeuvres with the army or navy or when we had to berth ships with just ourselves.

A large lifting vessel arrived one day called the *Swan*, and on her decks were two large barges. These barges were of the type used in the oil industry but they weren't loaded fore and aft they were spread from port to starboard, with about sixty feet overlapping each side of the *Swan*. Now no crane could have lifted these barges but apparently the *Swan* was capable of sinking herself so far like a submarine. These huge barges were then floated over the *Swan*. After securing the barges temporarily the *Swan* pumped out her ballast tanks and in doing so lifted herself, thus also raising the barges.

Dyvi Swan
Photo copyrights C. Noble.

However it was our job to take these barges off the *Swan* once they were floating again after the *Swan* had lowered herself again. It seemed amazing that a ship could sail 8000 miles with a cargo like that but it's the job she did regular and was built for.

These barges were to be used as a temporary jetty moored inside Stanley harbour, then ships could moor alongside them to discharge their cargoes. It worked similar to the Mulberry harbours that were used on D-Day during the 2nd World War in France.

It was very interesting work during my stay in the Falklands. At one time during army and navy manoeuvres we were to take twenty Ghurkhas and go around to San Carlos and land these Ghurkhas. They were sea sick and were glad to get off. They were supposed to be the enemy and likewise so was *Irishman.* I was told to hide myself and the Royal Navy was to try and find us and arrest us. So looking at the chart I found a very small inlet just big enough for a tug and also well sheltered from the weather. We ran lines to some rocks from our stern and put one anchor onto the bottom, turned our radar off and waited. Now any decent size ship couldn't do what we had done. We was laid like this for two days.

Through a crack in the cliff we often saw naval ships passing but came the day we were caught, not by a naval ship but a helicopter hovered above us and reported our position. Sure enough a rubber dingy with an outboard motor boarded us with marines on board and arrested the crew plus our cook, who was angry because he had been making some doughnuts. They made our crew lay spread eagled on the aft deck with rifles pointing at them. Me and the mate were kept on the bridge and questioned whilst a marine was pointing a revolver in our direction. I said to the navel officer "This is a fiddle because if we had been the real enemy we could have shot your helicopter down." However, war games over the naval officer said "How about some tea then?" Our cook, called Charlie Craft, said "You can all get stuffed because my doughnuts are ruined with you lot charging aboard."

Then on another occasion our job was to tow a floating target for the naval warships to practise their guns on. We used to tow the target about a mile astern, the frigates were out of sight but their shells were pretty accurate. One day we nearly had a hit aboard *Irishman,* in fact only about fifty feet away from us landed a shell. "Sorry about that," they said!

The Fridays were gash days, this meant that we went around every ship in the harbour to collect their rubbish, tons of it piled aboard. Then we had to steam out to sea three miles then dump the lot. I often wondered where this rubbish would finish up because it was in plastic bags. Wind and tide drifted the bags to the east and away from the Falkland Islands, mind you hundreds of sea gulls dived onto the bags because most of it was waste food etc.

After three long years we brought *Irishman* home again but it wasn't long before she was sold along with most of United's other sea going tugs. Then one day I was summoned to our office and politely told that I along with the other tug masters was being made redundant. In my case I could either be made redundant or I could transfer to Immingham across the Humber to join the river tugs, the choice was mine.

Chapter 12
1986 - Humber Tugs.

I thought about it, thinking working night and day doing river work like United Towing of old. So I said to this ex supply boat Captain who had never been on a tug, "If I take redundancy how much money would there be involved?" "Oh about £4000" came back the reply. I just said "Bye, bye I shall be joining Humber tugs."

So crossing the Humber I had an interview with Captain Sanderson of Humber Tugs and was given a three month trial. So going from tug to tug I was mainly just a spare skipper at first. If a skipper went off sick I would step in and take over until he came back. But the joy of it was that every tug in the Humber Tugs fleet had two crews, meaning that they all worked one week on and one week off, and also got paid for their week off. It was too good to be believed because with the old United Towing you came on and stayed on. What's more, if for instance you were ordered out for a dock or river job and another job turned up they called it a blue job - in other words 'a job out of the blue' then you got paid extra for doing it.

The biggest surprise was to come a few days before Christmas. I and other crew members were asked "Do you want to work Christmas?" I answered "Do I have a choice?" because up to joining Humber Tugs I'd never had a Christmas off for six years. My old mob in United used to send us out on so called salvage station over Christmas periods just so they wouldn't be disturbed and could have Christmas in peace.

After my three months probation was up I was accepted as a permanent master when a tug became available. I more or less got properly settled in with the job when Mr. Dalrimple, the Managing Director called me to his office. I was starting to get a bit worried now. Has something gone wrong or had they changed their mind, but I got a surprise, one I didn't really want.

The old guard, meaning United Towing, had asked my present boss if they could borrow me. Now I really started to get worried, here I was nicely settled in Humber Tugs, very comfortable. After my new boss explained to me what the job was going to be and that I would be coming back to Humber Tugs I felt better about it.

The war between Iran and Iraq was in full swing. Nothing to do with me you would think. It turned out that an Iranian jet fighter bomber had mistakenly attacked a Saudi Arabian oil tanker that had a British Master on board.

The tankers name was *Al Safaniya* and at the time of the attack the Master and Second Mate plus a steward were on the bridge of *Al Safaniya* watching the aircraft when, without warning, they sent a missile straight into *Al Safaniya's* wheelhouse killing everyone inside and causing a fire which the Arab crew managed to put out. This meant that *Al Safaniya* was drifting in the Persian Gulf and shouting for assistance

Al Safaniya
Photo copyright C. Noble.

An American tug called *Gulf Rambler* came to her rescue and took her in tow to the United Arab Emirates and, after patching *Al Safaniya* up and making her sea worthy got the contract to tow her to Singapore. The Captain of the *Gulf Rambler*, the tug chartered to tow her there, had no experience of ocean towing but they set off with *Al Safaniya* in tow. After several partings and *Al Safaniya* drifting for days she was eventually towed into Bombay where *Gulf Rambler's* Captain had refused to go any further and he went home!

After securing to *Al Safaniya* we set sail for Singapore. She towed well enough but food wise it was terrible. I just couldn't eat what they were eating. So raking around the food stores I found a case of tuna, also some Jacobs crackers and for a whole month that's what I lived on.

Charlie on the Gulf Rambler.
Copyright Capt. C. H. Noble

The *Gulf Rambler* was also alive with cockroaches. I remember one night turning my pillow over only to find hundreds of cockroaches squirming about. Hell I thought what the hell have I let myself into? I went down with diarrhoea and sickness but before arriving at Singapore I had recovered slightly and was keen to get ashore. A tug rep asked me if I would like a permanent job as Master of the *Gulf Rambler* - it was then that I found out that I could run. It turned out that the Salvage Association had requested my presence to do this job but now I knew what my answer would be in the future.

Gulf Rambler (1974)
Photo copyright unknown – Public domain.

Chapter 13
1996 - The Final Chapter. Retirement.

I returned back to the U.K. and was given a fortnights leave, and true to Humber Tug's word, returned back to my new job again. Better still I'd got my own tug called *Lady Debbie*, so now I was working in Immingham permanently.

Lady Debbie (1977)
Photo copyright unknown – Public domain.

We moved house from Hull to Immingham. I must admit, working with management and crews of Humber Tugs was the happiest time of all my tug career. Week on, week off, to me I was on cloud nine.

I spent almost ten years with Humber Tugs, my last tug being a tractor tug, brand new, called *Lady Josephine*. It was a pleasure just to be aboard of her and I was sorry to leave her when I finally retired.

I had a great send off by management and staff and was sorry to leave such a great bunch of men whom I shall never forget.

Charlie's last command, *Lady Josephine (1991)*
Photo copyright unknown – Public domain.